ISABELLA BIRD

A PHOTOGRAPHIC JOURNAL OF TRAVELS THROUGH CHINA 1894–1896

The Zig-Zag Bridge of Shanghai

"Its name indicates its peculiar character. It makes nine zig-zags across the water to the most celebrated tea house in Shanghai, and, perhaps, the most fashionable tea house in China. It is the resort of mandarins and people of the upper classes. Women are never seen at the tea houses. They are patronised by men only. Women, indeed, are very little seen in public at all. The absence of the female element is a marked feature in Chinese life."

1895

Gelatin silver print

10.7 x 15cm

Text from *Chinese Pictures: Notes on Photographs Made in China,* by Mrs J.F. Bishop FRGS

ISABELLA BIRD

A PHOTOGRAPHIC JOURNAL OF TRAVELS THROUGH CHINA 1894–1896

DEBORAH IRELAND

AMMONITE
PRESS

Royal
Geographical
Society
with IBG

Advancing geography
and geographical learning

First published 2015 by
Ammonite Press
an imprint of AE Publications Ltd
166 High Street, Lewes, East Sussex, BN7 1XU
United Kingdom

Text © Deborah Ireland, 2015
Foreword © Royal Geographical Society (with IBG), 2015
Images © Royal Geographical Society (with IBG), 2015
Copyright © in the Work AE Publications Ltd, 2015

ISBN 978-1-78145-097-0

British Library Cataloguing in Publication Data:
A catalogue record of this book is available from
the British Library.

Editor: Ian Penberthy
Managing Editor: Richard Wiles
Designer: Robin Shields
Publisher: Jonathan Bailey

Typeset in Helvetica Neue

Colour reproduction by GMC Reprographics
Printed in China

Disclaimer
The old Chinese place names and their spellings, quoted here, are those given by Isabella Bird herself in her book, *The Yangtze Valley and Beyond*. Many of them have changed long since (see page 235). It is possible, however, that due to the conditions under which she gathered her information, and because at the time she had no intention of publishing the material, some of them were recorded incorrectly, as she explains in the preface to that book:

"These journeys in China (concluding in 1897), of which the following pages are a record, were undertaken for recreation and interest solely, after some months of severe travelling in Korea. I had no intention of writing a book, and it was not till I came home, and China came very markedly to the front, and friends urged me that my impressions of the Yangtze Valley might be a useful contribution to popular knowledge of that much-discussed region, that I began to arrange my materials in their present form. They consist of journal letters, photographs, and notes from a brief diary.

"For a great part of my inland journey I have been unable to find any authorities to refer to, and as regards personal observation I agree sadly with the dictum of Socrates – 'The body is a hindrance to acquiring knowledge, and sight and hearing are not to be trusted.'

"I cannot hope to escape errors, but I have made a laborious effort to be accurate, and I trust and believe that they are not of material importance, and that in the main this volume will be found to convey a truthful impression of the country and its people.

"The spelling of place names needs an explanation. I have not the Chinese characters for them, and in many cases have only been able to represent by English letters the sounds as they reached my ear; but wherever possible, the transliteration given by Consul Playfair in his published list of Chinese Place Names* has been adopted, and with regard to a few well-known cities the familiar but unscholarly spelling has been retained."

The author and publisher have made great efforts to ensure that, to the best of their knowledge, all the images reproduced in this book were actually taken in China. Isabella Bird did not originally intend to publish a book on China, and as her prints came to the Society through her estate, the information on which countries a few of her images were taken in, from her travels in China, Japan and Korea, had become confused. Consequently, it is possible that a few were taken elsewhere in the region, for the inadvertent inclusion of which we apologise.

All quotes, excerpts, terms and opinions within this book are contemporary to the period in which they were originally made and should be viewed in their original cultural and historical context.

* *The Cities and Towns of China: a Geographical Dictionary* by George MacDonald Home Playfair, Foochow, 1879.

Rolex's long association with the Society dates from the 1930s and was celebrated in the first summiting of Everest in 1953. Today, Rolex supports the Society's unique photographic holdings and the wider care and conservation of its internationally important Collections relating to the history of exploration and travel.

Contents

Foreword

Isabella Lucy Bird was one of the most remarkable and high profile travellers of the Victorian age, with a reputation for tenacity and curiosity. She travelled widely in Canada, America, Hawaii, Japan, Malaysia, Persia, Kurdistan, Morocco, Tibet, Korea and China. Her travels began in 1854 and her last commenced in 1901. As a writer and photographer, she recounted her remarkable experiences to a devoted readership; whether climbing volcanoes or washing her photographic plates in the waters of the Yangtze. The Royal Geographical Society recorded in 1904 that 'she may be ranked with the most accomplished travellers of her time'. Isabella's achievements were all the more exceptional, given that they were set against the backdrop of lifelong illness, for which travel provided an antidote and distraction.

Isabella was one of the best-selling travel writers of her day, whose work was published by her friends at the company John Murray. As one of the Murray authors, her titles sat alongside books by David Livingstone and Charles Darwin. What distinguished her most from her peers was her ability to combine striking accounts of travel with the most engaging prose, later to be illustrated with her own photographs. Isabella Bird's audience devoured her books and appeared in huge crowds when she spoke publicly, eager to hear of her latest travels and experiences. She was recognised by the Society for 'her narratives, which embodied the results of much careful inquiry, and showed considerable power of insight into the political, moral, and religious conditions of the populations among which she moved'.

Isabella Bird came late to photography; but what she lacked in experience was made up in eager study. From 1886, and throughout her tenure as a Fellow, the Society had begun to promote the importance of photography to its Fellowship. The Society placed adverts within *The Geographical Journal* (the Society's primary scholarly publication at the time) to remind its readers of the importance of the medium and appointed John Thomson as its 'Instructor in Photography'. This beginning enabled the Society to create one of the finest collections of photography, which provides a unique visual record of the world from 1850 to the present day.

Within this extensive, internationally-recognised archive – which includes works by photographers such as Carleton Watkins, Herbert Ponting and Alfred Gregory – Isabella Bird's prints are particularly valued not only for their aesthetic quality, but also for the careful, thoughtful and sensitive way in which she approached her subjects. Isabella undoubtedly had a gift for photography. In a letter dated 23rd January, 1897 to John Murray IV she confessed 'nothing ever took such hold of me as Photography has done. If I felt sure to follow my inclination I should give my whole time to it.' Her images of China, combined with her text, present one of the earliest photojournalistic accounts of China at the end of the nineteenth century. It is for this reason that her collection of prints sits at the very heart of the Society's photographic collection today. I am delighted to see her photographs of China revisited in such a compelling way here in this new book. I do hope you enjoy learning more about this remarkable woman and her travels.

Dr Rita Gardner CBE
Director, Royal Geographical Society (with IBG)

Left: Portrait of Isabella Bird taken in Edinburgh by Elliot & Fry.

Bridge and temple in Puto, Chusan Archipelago

"The group of sacred buildings, embowered in rich foliage, and backed by the granite-topped hill, the bright colours of the roofs and walls, the sacred lotus lake spanned by a bridge of marble, together make up a picture of rare, romantic beauty."

1895

Gelatin silver print

11.1 x 15cm

Text from *Illustrations of China and its People, Volume III*, by John Thomson

Introduction

Isabella Bird: A Photographic Journal of Travels Through China aims to explain why such an established and successful travel writer would embark on photography with such vigour and enthusiasm in the latter part of her life. It explores what inspired her to become so accomplished and to persuade her publisher, John Murray, to use her photographs.

It is very fitting that the Royal Geographical Society (with IBG) should produce a book to highlight the Chinese photographic work of Isabella Lucy Bird (Mrs J.F. Bishop) FRGS held in its historic photographic collection.

Her journeys in China were the first that she made where creating a photographic record of a place was her prime aim. Her photographs show China on the cusp of change and under pressure from foreign influence. After arriving unplanned and unprepared in 1894, she returned frequently over a three-year period, fascinated by the order and way of life in China, its culture and its people. The country continued to draw her back, to absorb and delight her. It was only when she returned home that pressure from friends prompted her to write about her experiences. The resulting book was *The Yangtze Valley and Beyond*, which was published by John Murray in 1899.

In the history of photography, it is unusual to have such a detailed record of the working practices of a travel photographer active at this time, often improvising in the most difficult of circumstances to create negatives and photographs successfully. She recorded failures as well as her successes, and it is this approach that gives such a good insight into how she worked.

The photographs in this book are presented together for the first time to show the journeys she made in 1894, 1895 and 1896. The written accounts of her time in China appeared in *Korea and Her Neighbours* (1898), *The Yangtze Valley and Beyond* (1899) and *Chinese Pictures* (1900). These books form the main source of the captions we have used to accompany Isabella's photographic plates.

Isabella Bird: A Photographic Journal of Travels Through China is a celebration of a remarkable woman, who made her mark in a male-dominated world of travel and photography, at a time when both were fraught with many difficulties.

Deborah Ireland

A Traveller's Tales

Isabella Bird taken just before her marriage in 1881 by J. Moffat.

sabella Bird was a wonderful writer who could engage the imagination. She took her readers along with her to the islands of Hawaii, galloping on horseback, climbing volcanoes, crossing the paths of grizzly bears in California and, of course, meeting the desperado Rocky Mountain Jim. *The Spectator* said of her:

"There was never anybody who had adventures as well as Miss Bird." [1]

The book that brought her fame and fortune was *The Hawaiian Archipelago: Six Months Among the Palm Groves, Coral Reefs and Volcanoes of the Sandwich Islands,* published in 1875. It was based on descriptive letters that she had sent to her sister, Henrietta, from Hawaii. Writing to her in 1873, Isabella suggested that she should read the letters 'like a book'[2] to her assembled friends back home. The friends' response was so positive that the idea was planted of reaching a wider audience, so she wrote to her publisher, John Murray III, suggesting an edited version of the letters for publication.[3]

Isabella was already an experienced writer, having produced a self-published pamphlet on free trade when she was just seventeen.[4] From that point on, she wrote continuously, her first book, *The Englishwoman in America,* being published in 1856 by John Murray. The book sold reasonably well, but it was the style that she developed while working on the Hawaiian letters, and her editing and honing of the text to create a vivid narrative, that made her popular with the public. More than just an adventure story, it was packed with interesting nuggets of information, descriptions of flora and fauna and geographical detail, presented in an easy-to-read form. In all her subsequent writing, there was a fair amount of tantalising gore and fascinating asides to

keep the reader turning the pages. Her books were engaging, accessible and entertaining, and she opened up a world of travel and geography to the armchair explorer, making it fun.

Writing sustained her, especially through crippling spinal pain, giving her freedom and a channel for her creativity. Best of all, it helped reshape her identity, provided financial support and instilled in her a formidable inner confidence. As *The Spectator* put it in a review of *A Lady's Life in the Rocky Mountains:*

"… a most encouraging record of feminine confidence and masculine chivalrousness".[5]

The adventuress who travelled and rode in all weathers, exploring remote and dangerous regions, was writing about a life in sharp contrast to the one originally envisaged for her. Isabella had been born in 1831, into a relatively wealthy, religious family. During her younger life, her father, the Reverend Edward Bird, moved progressively to parishes with smaller stipends, his dwindling income being subsidised by inherited money. In 1848, the family moved to Wyton, Huntingdon, where they lived in reasonable comfort. They were wealthy enough for Isabella to have a horse and ride with the hunt. There was also enough income to fund her travel to America in 1854, aged 23, for her health and to mend a broken heart or, as she put it:

"… circumstances which it is unnecessary to dwell upon led me across the Atlantic with some relatives."

As well as completing *The Englishwoman in America,* on her return she also wrote for various journals, including the *North America Review.*

Isabella's life changed abruptly two years later, in 1858, when her father died of influenza, forcing the

"There was never anybody who had adventures as well as Miss Bird."

Isabella's Hawaiian riding dress: "a thoroughly serviceable and feminine costume".

mothers, and unmarried women were often viewed as failures. The wealth and status of women were shaped by their menfolk. Social standing was determined by the profession of a woman's father until marriage, and then by that of her husband. In the pecking order of the time, a spinster fell below the rank of widow. It is interesting that Isabella, without a father or brother, expected John Murray III to take on the role of protector and defender of her honour. In 1879, when the reviewer in *The Times* wrote, 'She donned masculine habiliments for greater convenience',[8] she expected John Murray III to horsewhip the fellow.[9] A more practical resolution was found by including an illustration of Isabella's Hawaiian riding dress, accompanied by the following note to the second edition:

"For the benefit of other lady travellers, I wish to explain that my 'Hawaiian riding dress' is the 'American Lady's Mountain Dress', a half-fitting jacket, a skirt reaching to the ankles, and full Turkish trousers gathered into frills which fall over the boots – a thoroughly serviceable and feminine costume for mountaineering and other rough travelling in any part of the world. I add this explanation to the prefatory note, together with a rough sketch of the costume, in consequence of an erroneous statement in *The Times* of November 22nd."

family to quit the rectory. Mother and both daughters eventually settled into a flat in Castle Terrace, Edinburgh. For a girl used to wide horizons, travel and a home in a country rectory, moving to the upper floor of a rented city flat was a marked change of status and something of a challenge. When the girls' mother, Dora, died in 1866, she left £3,346[6] to be divided equally between them. While for most at the time, this would have seemed a wonderfully generous sum, for the two sisters, raised to enjoy a certain standard of life, it was quite a restrictive amount. It would have to sustain them for the rest of their lives, however, as at the ages of thirty-four and thirty, they were spinsters with little prospect of marriage. In the 1850s, marriage rates dropped drastically for spinsters over the age of thirty.[7] In fact, a woman was far more likely to marry if she were a widow, such as Isabella's friend from Wyton days, Fanny Puckle, who remarried and emigrated to Australia.

Today it is difficult to grasp the situation in which widows and spinsters found themselves during the Victorian and Edwardian eras. Young middle-class women were expected to become good wives and

Religious faith provided a comfort in bleak times. Being related to the Wilberforce family (anti-slavery campaigner William Wilberforce was a founding member of the Church Missionary Society), the Birds had a great tradition of religious duty and service. As children, their summers were spent at the paternal family home at Taplow Hill, Buckinghamshire, where the extended family gathered, including cousins whose parents were missionaries abroad. There was a strict evangelical regime of daily prayers and lessons before breakfast, followed by the reading aloud of letters, with more readings and singing in the evening. Good causes and helping others provided comfort and distraction after their father's death. When the family settled in Edinburgh, both sisters became involved with schemes to help starving West Highlanders (victims of the Highland clearances and failing crops)[10] and draw attention to the condition of Edinburgh slums.[11]

After her initial success with *The Englishwoman in America*, Isabella wrote mainly on religious subjects and for journals such as *The Leisure Hour, The Family Treasury, Good Words* and *Sunday at Home*.[12] She also wrote in support of favourite causes, such as the slim volume *Notes on Old Edinburgh*,[13] published in 1869, which exposed the living conditions in the city's slums; it made harrowing reading.

At this time, much of Isabella's energy was expended in working on quite tough and exhausting subjects, so it is little wonder that she was dogged by depression and poor health. In 1872, in an attempt to achieve a rest cure, her doctors suggested the climate of Australia, where fortunately there were friends with whom she could stay, including the aforementioned Fanny Puckle. Unfortunately the trip proved to be something of a disaster.

The journey to Australia was grim. Isabella was ill, felt homesick and lonely, and hated the heat. She wrote in desperation to Henrietta from Melbourne, indicating her intention to abandon the plan and return to Edinburgh. In these Australian letters, money and status were very much a concern, and she proposed taking a house with Henrietta on her return:

"I want it taken on again and I will pay the rent out of my own savings … we have not money enough to get it in a good situation and the WCs of flats are so objectionable."[14]

Later she began to rally, but was still concerned about the lack of money. While staying with her old friend Fanny Puckle in Victoria, she writes:

"I had forgotten how much I had ridden with her [Fanny Puckle] when I had the money."[15]

It is in this letter, outlining her route home via California and the Rocky Mountains, that she proposed working as a servant (see display quote). Also, incidentally, it would have provided her with some great copy. However, it was on this return journey that she stopped in Hawaii and her fortunes changed forever. From then on, she concentrated on writing travel narratives, her books were never out of print and she received an annual income from John Murray Publishers for the rest of her life. After the print run of *The Hawaiian Archipelago* sold out in the first year, she renegotiated her publishing deal with John Murray III from half to three-quarters in her favour, which was extraordinary for the time. Her work was serialised in magazines, and published both in the UK and the USA. Her bestselling titles were *The Hawaiian Archipelago* (1875), *A Lady's Life in the Rocky Mountains* (1879) and *Unbeaten Tracks in Japan* (1880).

What made Isabella different from contemporary travel writers was the quality of her prose; still a joy

"… manual labour, a rough life and freedom from conventionalities added to novelty would be a good thing."

to read today. There is a timelessness and lightness of touch; information is absorbed effortlessly as you turn the page. The description of her journey across the Rockies includes her relationship with the horse she rides; she takes you with her on the cattle drives. It is pure Wild West adventure. She had been writing for twenty-eight years before she found the style that worked for her, but once she had found it, she was unstoppable.

Although Isabella had already proved to be a competent travel writer by the age of twenty-five, in the intervening years she gained maturity, experience and command over her text. Educated at home, she was well read and had a good knowledge of contemporary literature. Books such as James Fenimore Cooper's *The Last of the Mohicans*[16] inspired her to call her horse Mohawk, and this may have led her to dream of America as a young girl. In maturity, George Eliot was one of her favourite authors,[17] and in a letter to Henrietta[18] she described delivering an edition of *Middlemarch*[19] to Mrs Hutchinson in Big Thompson Canyon, Colorado, a shocking journey during which her hands froze to her reins, her eyelids froze together and her horse Birdie became festooned with ice crystals. She was also familiar with the work of other travel writers.

Books such as *Travels in North America 1827–1828*, by Basil Hall,[20] and *Domestic Manners of America* by Frances Trollope,[21] 1832, were almost certainly familiar to Isabella. The accounts of slavery and attitudes to religion would have been studied during the summer months at Taplow Hill, 'where the ladies of the family took no sugar in their tea, and felt the sacrifice to be a sacred protest against slave-grown products.'[22]

Isabella does stress in the preface that she gives impressions in her writing rather than drawing conclusions. In contrast, Trollope's *Domestic Manners of America* was famous for its harsh criticism and exaggeration of some aspects of the American way of life; it became an instant bestseller. However, one lesson Isabella may have picked up from Trollope and employed subsequently in her own writing was that a bit of hardship sells books:

"The nights were insupportable. We used to lounge on the bow, and retire late at night to our cabins, to fight the heat, and scare rats and kill cockroach with our slippers."[23]

Isabella also read around her subject, adding extra text and information. Henrietta, her inspiration and the recipient of her letters, and to whom she affectionately dedicated her books, appears to have contributed additional information. Kay Chubbuck, in her book *Letters to Henrietta*,[24] draws attention to a letter written in 1889, in which Isabella describes how her sister helped with additional research:

"One thing out of many which made my letters to her what they were was the singular amount of her accumulated knowledge of countries, of their geography, products, government, ethnology, religions and botany. She always read and took notes of the best travels, comparing them with naturalists and other books on the same subjects."[25]

Henrietta was Isabella's touchstone; she also sought her sister's opinion on publishing her work:

"I want to know if you think Edmonston and Douglas would like to publish my travels *Ten months in the Pacific*? My island tour would do for 'Good Words' not the Sunday Magazine. It would be much better for me to publish it there and afterwards as a book."[26]

"I seem to have so much to say now and writing travels is not hard brain work."

Isabella in Colorado in her riding outfit and with her horse Birdie.

Isabella's uniqueness as a traveller was recognised by George Curzon, Royal Geographical Society Council member, in his letter to *The Times* of 30th May, 1893, in reaction to the ongoing debate about women Fellows at the Royal Geographical Society. She was in the first group of fifteen women to be made Fellows (by 1892, she had married and been widowed, so is mentioned as Mrs Bishop):

"We contest in toto the general capability of women to contribute to scientific geographical knowledge. Their sex and training render them equally unfitted for exploration: and the general professional female globe-trotters with which America has lately familiarised us is one of the horrors of the latter end of the 19th century. In our teeth are thrown the names of one or two distinguished ladies, such as Mrs Bishop, whose additions to geographical knowledge have been valuable and serious. But in the whole of England these ladies can be counted on the fingers of one hand: and in the entire range of modern geography I question if history will preserve the names of half that number."[28]

And later:

"You should propel me to people who will get me employment to write, for I seem to have so much to say now and writing travels is not hard brain work."[27]

The death of Henrietta in 1880 was a huge loss. Isabella's later travels and her books were more in the style of reportage, serious in tone and approach. She did eventually get married in 1881, to surgeon Dr John Bishop, but after only five years he died of pernicious anaemia. To honour the memory of both her sister and husband, Isabella set up two hospitals during a spell in India, but the sadness of this time never really left her.

As a respected international traveller, her views were sought by prime ministers, ambassadors and the newspapers of the day. By the time she took up photography, her international reputation was firmly established.

Curzon did change his mind twenty years later regarding women's contribution to geography, and while Isabella always regarded him as a friend, she could not resist a joke at his expense when writing to John Scott Keltie, the secretary of the Royal Geographical Society, on her return from China in 1897:

"I hear myself so continually spoken of as 'the distinguished traveller' that I am arriving at the very same natural conclusion that I am as well entitled to a medal as Mr Curzon or some others!!"[29]

A Passion for Photography

Snapshot taken of Mrs Bishop at Swatow by Mr Mackenzie

ISABELLA BIRD

Photography became an 'intense pleasure'[1] for Isabella Bird and was something she pursued even under very challenging conditions. She describes the feeling photography gave her in a letter to her publisher, John Murray, written as she was preparing to return home from the Far East in 1897:

"I must confess that nothing ever took such a hold of me as photography has done. If I felt sure to follow my inclinations I should give my whole time to it."[2]

The joy she experienced when creating a photographic print was something she wanted to share with others, regardless of rank or status, from the itinerant trackers employed to haul her boat up the Yangtze rapids, who initially thought she kept a black devil in the camera,[3] to members of the Church Mission Society with whom she stayed, using their guest bedrooms as improvised darkrooms.[4]

The person responsible for Isabella's introduction to photography was Sir John Scott Keltie, secretary of the Royal Geographical Society.[5] Keltie was a Scot with a background in publishing, working primarily for Macmillan and Co., where he was a sub-editor on *Nature* from 1873,[6] with responsibility for geography and education. *Nature*, still published today, was a weekly journal of science, with illustrated accounts being one of its original mission statements. As secretary of the Royal Geographical Society, Keltie had a happy knack of befriending explorers and preserving a harmonious atmosphere in the Society.[7] A genuine friendship existed between Keltie and Isabella, and when she was proposed for fellowship of the Royal Geographical Society by John

Murray IV, Keltie was the seconder.[8] Isabella credits Keltie with starting her on photography in a letter she sent to him dated 10th March, 1897, while aboard the P&O steamer *Formosa* in Valetta, Malta, on her return journey from China:

"As you originally put me in the way of getting me a camera and started on photographing through Mr Thomson, you may be interested to hear that I am bringing back 1,200 photographs."[9]

The Mr Thomson to whom Isabella refers is John Thomson, the Scottish travel photographer of the Far East, who is credited with being the first photojournalist.[10] In 1886, Thomson was appointed Instructor of Photography at the Royal Geographical Society.[11] His brief was to give advice on photography to the leading explorers of the day.

It is possible to gain an understanding of the probable content covered in the lessons given to Isabella by John Thomson from the photography section of the Royal Geographical Society publication *Hints to Travellers*,[12] a guide that provided information on everything a traveller would be likely to need. John Thomson updated the photography section, which dealt with the latest equipment, chemicals

John Scott Keltie, firm friend of Isabella and secretary of the Royal Geographical Society.

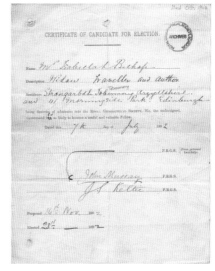

Isabella's certificate of candidate for election to the Royal Geographical Society.

and processing techniques. From suppliers to storage, everything was covered in detail to enable the 'traveller-photographer' to achieve successful photographs. The guide stressed the need for professional operators to study for years. This may be why in June, 1892, at the age of 61, Isabella took additional instruction in photography from Howard Farmer, head of photography at Regent Street Polytechnic,[13] and continued with lessons from time to time when she was in London. She also took lessons in Edinburgh in 1893, learning how to make prints from her own film negatives.[14]

In *Hints to Travellers*, Thomson explained that the aim for all travel photographers was the production of good negatives. He stressed the advantages of developing a few plates during a long journey, both as tests for exposure and to prove that all the apparatus was in order. He also suggested that generally it was best to get the printing done by a professional printer. Isabella seems to have developed all her negatives while she travelled, and she also made a considerable number of prints, even toning them, in the most basic conditions. In a letter to John Murray, regarding a lost box of negatives and her joy at its rediscovery, she mentions her disappointment in the quality of prints made from her negatives while in Japan:

"I think many are capable of being improved and it is certainly possible to get far better prints from all than the Japanese photographers have produced."[15]

Her ability to produce high-quality negatives in the field gives an indication of the level of Isabella's skills. She could produce film negatives with great success, and was using them in the rarefied air on the slopes around the village of Mia-ko, where the celluloid films emitted sparks when they were separated.[16]

"I must confess that nothing ever took such a hold of me as photography has done."

Thomson explains the pros and cons of both glass and film negative types:

"Without doubt, glass plates yield the best results; but celluloid films in the smaller sizes up to 7½ x 5, approach very nearly to glass in many respects, and have the advantage of being one twelfth the weight and not liable to breakage. They are exposed in the same slides, and require the same treatment as glass plates. As, however, the production of good film negatives requires considerable skill and nicety of manipulation, it will be well for the traveller who has not been able to attain expertness therein, to provide himself with glass plates in addition to flat celluloid films."[17]

Isabella used a combination of celluloid film and glass-plate negatives.[18] Thomson recommended taking two cameras,[19] one of them handheld to supplement the work of a larger instrument, and Isabella followed his advice. Her equipment comprised a Ross camera with tripod, 'one of Ross's best', weighing 16lb, and a hand camera weighing 4lb.[20]

We get a good understanding of how she worked from her own account in *The Yangtze Valley and Beyond*, where she describes producing prints and negatives in different situations. Between Hankow and Ichang, she was on an American-built stern-wheel steamer. She described the captain as kind and genial, but prone to using bad language, even in front of women and clergy. Nonetheless, he was very accommodating:

"He let me tone unlimited photographic prints in the saloon, ignoring the dishes and buckets involved in the process, and the engineer provided an unlimited supply of condensed water, free from both Yangtze mud and from alum used to precipitate it."[21]

Two lantern slides created from Isabella's photographic plates in 1896 and used to illustrate her talks. The slide on the left shows men carrying wine in special baskets; the slide on the right depicts a double-roofed bridge. The original images were reproduced in her book, *The Yangtze Valley and Beyond*.

However, it was not quite so easy on the small houseboat she shared with the boatman's family and the trackers employed to drag the boat up the rapids between Ichang and Wan Hsien. Here she describes how she passed her time in the evenings after a full day's travelling:

"... above all, there were photographic negatives to develop and print, and prints to tone, and the difficulties enhanced the zest of these processes and made me think, with a feeling of complacent superiority, of the amateurs who need 'dark rooms', sinks, water 'laid on', tables, and other luxuries. Night supplied me with a dark room; the majestic Yangtze was 'laid on'; a box served for a table: all else can be dispensed with.

"I lined my 'stall' with muslin curtains and newspapers, and finding the light of the opium lamps still came in through the chinks, I tacked up my blanket and slept in my clothes and fur coat. With 'water, water everywhere', water was the great

difficulty. The Yangtze holds any amount of fine mud in suspension, which for drinking purposes is usually precipitated with alum, and unless filtered, deposits a fine, even veil on the negative. I had only a pocket filter, which produced about three quarts of water a day, of which Be-dien [her interpreter] invariably abstracted some for making tea, leaving me with only enough for a final wash, not always quite effectual, as the critic will see from some of the illustrations.

"I found that the most successful method of washing out 'hypo' was to lean over the gunwale and hold the negative in the wash of the Great River, rapid even at the mooring place, and give it some final washes in the filtered water. This chilly arrangement was only possible when the trackers were ashore or smoking opium at the stern. Printing was a great difficulty, and I only overcame it by hanging the printing-frames over the side. When all these rough arrangements were successful, each print was a joy and a triumph, nor was there disgrace in failure."[22]

The Church Mission House at Shao-Hsing, where Isabella stayed with the Reverend W. Gilbert Walshe: "I had the honour of entertaining Mrs Bishop for a short period at Shao-Hsing. She proposed to stay for a night only; but finding the city and neighbourhood full of interest, she consented to prolong her visit for nearly a week. It was characteristic of her spirit of independence that she declined all offer of escort…"

"… retiring at night about 11p.m. apparently quite worn out; but always had sufficient reserves of strength to occupy an extra hour or two in the development of her photographs."[24]

Protecting her equipment as she travelled was a major concern for Isabella. Early in her Korean exploration, she lost negatives when her boat was swamped by rapids.[25] After that experience, she always took great care to prevent such a disaster from happening again. Later, when ascending rapids on the Yangtze:

The practice of working on her photographs in the evenings, using the night sky as her darkroom, was something Isabella also did when she toured the church missions during 1895. During this journey, she stayed with Dr and Mrs Main as a guest of the Church Missionary Society, in Hangchow. Mrs Main described how she received her first lesson in photography from Isabella:

"She was the most enthusiastic photographer yielding to the fascination and excitement of developing her plates and toning her prints at night, midnight and even early morning. She gave me my first lesson in photography, and was as pleased as could be to teach me how to develop, which she told me in the 'dark room' was the most interesting part of it all."[23]

Isabella also stayed with the Reverend W. Gilbert Walshe in Shao-Hsing. He described her visit as being very interesting, noting that she was an easy guest to entertain:

"My preparations were to pack my plates, films, and general photographic outfit, journals, a few necessaries, and a few things of fictitious value, in a waterproof bag, to be carried by my servant, along with my camera, at each rapid where we landed."[26]

On land, she carried her cameras in a compartment under the seat of her travelling chair,[27] and there she managed to preserve them in good order when her other possessions where spoiled or damaged by the harshness of the terrain and elements she endured on her journeys.

So why did Isabella take up photography so late in life, and at a time when she was already an established author and traveller? The answer is partly because photographs could be used as a visual record – a memory prompter to supplement the diary she kept of her travels. But overwhelmingly there was the very practical reason of an increasing need for illustrative material for both lectures and books.

Isabella was travelling in remote, uncharted areas, and she had great difficulty in finding material that would accurately reflect what she saw unless she created it herself. This was particularly true of China, where the great diversity of the culture meant that if you missed taking an image because of weather or lack of time, you would never see anything like it again; the opportunity would be lost.[28]

As a speaker, she was an accomplished orator and could draw crowds of up to two thousand to her lectures.[29] She was aware of the impact good illustrations could make on an audience and was experienced at using lantern slides with her talks. A review in *The Times*, from November, 1891, of a talk she gave at the Royal Scottish Geographical Society, describes how it was illustrated with a series of views shown by the limelight (lime was used, in pellet form, to illuminate the magic lantern by burning it with oxygen and hydrogen).[30]

The Royal Geographical Society had purchased such a lantern in 1890 for illustrating its evening lectures.[31] This was after much initial debate, as some members thought it would 'lower the Society's discussion to the level of a Sunday School treat with a magic lantern.'[32] By the time Isabella had returned from China in 1897, the Society had appointed a member of staff to assist speakers with the making of lantern slides[33] and also loaned slides to members for the illustration of their talks.[34]

Isabella also used photographic prints during less formal talks, such as the one she gave to the people of Tobermory at Christmas in 1891. There she displayed photographs as well as sketches, and persuaded two members of the YWCA to dress in Persian costume. The talk was titled 'Persia and the Persians', and she records that the audience was:

"Delirious with enthusiasm and delight and the vote of thanks was a wild highland uproar of stamping, clapping, hurraring and waving of hats and handkerchiefs."[35]

But the driving force that got her 'started on photographing through Mr Thomson' was the need for true-to-life 'faithfull'[36] illustrations for her own publications. From the outset, she was influenced by a photographer who was the master of the published photograph and the printing techniques of the time. John Thomson was six years younger than Isabella, but he had begun publishing his own work well before she embarked on her life-changing journey to Australia. In 1866, he visited the ancient temples of Angkor Wat, publishing his photographs in a book, *The Antiquities of Cambodia*,[37] the following year. The albumen photographs that illustrated the book were physically pasted into each copy. However, later publications of his photography employed a variety of photomechanical processes.

Significantly for Isabella, Thomson had also travelled and worked in China between 1868 and 1871, and his *Illustrations of China and Its People*,[38] a four-volume publication that appeared in 1873 and 1874, was illustrated with collotypes, similar to a modern publication process, which enabled both image and text to be printed on a single sheet of paper. This greatly speeded up the compiling of books illustrated with images, but it was very expensive, and a year later, Thomson brought out *The Straits of Malacca, Indo-China and China*,[39] a much cheaper publication illustrated with engravings taken from his original photographs.

"She was the most enthusiastic photographer yielding to the fascination and excitement of developing her plates and toning her prints at night, midnight and even early morning."

John Thomson and Isabella both photographed the ancient astrological instruments at the Peking Observatory (left and right respectively). These photographs show their different approaches. John Thomson's experience provides him with an instinctive understanding of how to get the most out of subjects, editing out any distractions from the shot. What Isabella lacks in experience she makes up for in enthusiasm, and of course she was developing her own style.

Thomson was in a unique position at the Royal Geographical Society: not only could he give advice to explorers and travellers on the best way to secure images of what they saw and discovered, but also he could draw on his own experience to advise how photography could best be translated into print.

In a letter warning John Murray of delays in returning to England and submitting text for her next publication – 'consequently my Korean book cannot be a Xmas book unfortunately' – Isabella broaches the subject of using her own photographs:

"Illustrations by a cheap process seem a great feature in books of travel now. I don't think that I mentioned that I have a number of my own photographs for this purpose, negatives I mean."[40]

Writing from Japan three months later, in July, 1896, she tells John Murray that as so many people want copies of her photographs, she intends to self-publish fifty of her own images in a book, using the collotype process:[41]

"It seems essential now to illustrate somewhat profusely by means of reproductions of photographs after somewhat fuzzy photogravures or collotypes I think. I wondered if by my combined efforts it could be brought out at Easter?"[42]

The publication of a book was a practical way of supplying images to friends[43] without losing her carefully crafted prints. One volume of photographs was produced to help raise money for a hospital.[44] Published in 1897, a small, slim volume entitled *Views in the Far East*, published by S. Kajima of Tokyo, contained images of China, Japan and Korea.[45]

Korea and Her Neighbours, a two-volume edition, was eventually published by John Murray in 1898. It contained a mix of engravings and 'fuzzy photogravures'. John Murray arranged for the engraver, Whymper, to use Isabella's photographs as a basis for his line drawings, and she was delighted with the results.[46] However, when *The Yangtze Valley and Beyond* was published a year later, it was illustrated with 106 of Isabella's own images, reproduced as photographs and marking a complete change from her previous publications. In 1900, *Chinese Pictures* was published by Cassell and Co., a book of forty-one photographs with expanded captions. In four years, Isabella had published four books. As soon as one book was completed, she began work on another, leaving little time for reflection or rest.

Today, Isabella's photographs seem like carefully-crafted jewels. The majority are 10.5 x 15cm,[47] and they are beautiful examples of toning and enamelling, the techniques she describes so well. She photographed places, people and how people lived. When there was time to set up a shot, the compositions are carefully considered, but often the image is a straight record of a place, with the subject set square in the centre of the frame.

Many of the places Isabella visited during her three years in China were also locations photographed by John Thomson and published in his book *Illustrations of China and its People*. She seemed to have used his work as a guide for her own exploration, particularly in 1895. Working over twenty years apart, however, they used very different photographic processes and equipment. What they shared was a photo-journalistic approach and an exploration of the detail of people's lives and their society. Some of Isabella's shots appear to have been set up with the same viewpoint as Thomson's. It seems likely that she was familiar with his work, even prior to having lessons in photography from him. Both were well-known, published authors, and both received glowing reviews of their books in *Nature* in 1875,[48] most probably written by John Scott Keltie.

Isabella often captured more than just the subject, providing an intriguing view of the place in which she was travelling. It's the incidental inclusion of ship sterns and people peering out from buildings

that enriches the general picture. Perhaps the most astounding thing is that she was able to create such carefully-crafted negatives in such hostile and, at times, even combative conditions. The rough treatment she received in Szechuan caused concussion and shook her nerves, but did not deter her:

"The whole scene is beautiful and it was most mortifying that the crowd which gathered round my camera, looking in at the lens and over my shoulder under the focusing cloth and shaking it violently, prevented me from getting a picture of it".[49]

Staying at a country inn, she was frustrated at night while trying to develop her negatives when they were fogged by a flash of light from a curious neighbour, who had worked a hole through the wall of her bedroom.[50]

Isabella was realistic about her skill as a photographer. She was confident in her technical ability, regarding her negatives as 'faithfull though not artistic'.[51] To improve her artistic capability, she joined the Royal Photographic Society in 1897,[52] providing her with the opportunity to study the 'art and science of photography,' as she expressed to John Scott Keltie:

"I am almost ashamed to say that photography has become a complete craze. I like it better than any pursuit I ever undertook and if I should ever have time to give to the techniques of the art, I hope to improve considerably."[53]

"I am almost ashamed to say that photography has become a complete craze."

A Chinese Odyssey

MAP OF
CHINA
PREPARED FOR
THE CHINA INLAND MISSION
1899.

- - - 1894

- - - 1895

- - - 1896

Isabella Bird made three forays into China in the years 1894, 1895 and 1896, at a time of her life when she had expected to give up the rigours of exploration travel.

At the beginning of the 1890s, China was vulnerable to foreign powers who wished to expand into and exploit its markets and territories.[1] The country's reluctance to 'modernise' and adopt Western ideas was in sharp contrast to Japan, which had undergone great change and was looking for opportunities to extend its influence.[2]

Known as the Hermit Kingdom because of its closed policy to outsiders, Korea had relied for centuries on China to defend its borders, but this changed in 1884 when a convention between Japan and China reduced Korea to a virtual co-protectorate of the two countries. Lying between China and Japan, Korea would become the battleground for future tensions in the area.[3]

Setting off from Liverpool on 11th January, 1894,[4] Isabella Bird was unaware that she was heading straight into a war zone, or that she would spend the next three years absorbed by travel in China, Japan and Korea, having told her publisher the year before that she was too old for the discomforts of exploration travel.

Isabella would spend those years in the Far East with her camera developing a deep fascination for China, after what can only be described as a calamitous introduction. Unprepared and without any plans, funds or baggage, in 1894 she was forced by the British vice-consul at the Korean port of Chemulpo to board a Japanese steamer bound for China. The presence of recently-arrived Japanese troops in the port was the cause of much concern and had prompted his action, as Isabella commented:

"… a state that may be mildly termed having 'lost his head.'"[6]

She returned in 1895 for a much more relaxed and leisurely tour of Protestant missions and the Chusan Archipelago, and again in 1896 to explore the Yangtze and beyond.

In 1894, her original intention had been to travel to Yokohama, Japan, and use it as a base to visit Korea. She was very familiar with Japan, having first travelled there in 1878. The country was very different in character to its near neighbours, having begun a programme of modernisation. By the 1890s, it had a modern army and navy, and a fast growing industrial base.[7] It was also a comfortable country for a Western traveller, with hotels and mountain resorts for rest and recuperation.

After a relatively short stay in Kobe, Japan, Isabella began her exploration of Korea. She started with Seoul and was desperately disappointed, finding it monotonous and drab. She doubted that it would make an interesting subject for a book, but the situation began to improve when she explored the Han River and found great beauty in the landscape. She concluded this first journey at Won-san, a port on the east side of the country, and decided to use it as a future base, leaving her travelling equipment behind with the intention of returning for it in the autumn, after the rainy season.

Rumours were circulating in Won-san of a conflict between a rebel group known as the Tong-haks, and the Korean Royal Army. The Tong-haks were against Western influence in the south of Korea and were supported by oppressed peasant farmers. Isabella

"I am thinking of going to pay a few visits in Japan next winter, and may possibly go on to Korea; but I am too old for hardships and great exertions now."[5]

did not attach much importance to the rumours and took a boat around the south of Korea to the port of Chemulpo, not imagining that the fighting would affect her in any way. Unfortunately, this was not the case:

"The war maimed my plan and left me with a mutilated half. I reached Chemulpo on June 21 by steamer intending to go to Seoul, get my money and my luggage and in a few days go to Japan for the summer. I found Chemulpo occupied by the Japanese and was ordered away that night not into a position of security, but actually into the lion's mouth, i.e. on board a Japanese steamer, which sailed that night for the ports in the Gulf of Pechili! I was penniless, and had only the clothes I wore, and in this state reached Chefoo where the Consul provided me with money, and the wives of the British and Spanish Ministry made up a bundle of under clothing. On their kindness I subsisted through the long hot summer."[8]

There was good reason for alarm at Chemulpo. In the outer harbour, there were six Japanese warships, an American flagship, two French ships, a Russian ship and two ships of the Chinese fleet. In the inner harbour, Japanese transports were ferrying troops, horses and war materials to the shore. Within two hours of arriving, the Japanese had set up a camp of 1,200 men under canvas, complete with stables. Isabella described visiting the camp accompanied by a young Russian officer and watching dinner being served in lacquered boxes.[9] A total of 6,000 Japanese troops with provisions for three months were landed; their intentions were unclear. Concern was spreading among the Chinese residents of Chemulpo, and with the arrival of

A group of Chinese medical students at the mission hospital in Mukden, the second city of the Chinese empire, where Isabella recovered from illness and a broken arm suffered when her cart overturned.

the troops, they decided it was time to leave.

Isabella was mortified by the experience, describing it as a blow. She took great pride in looking after herself, managing her own affairs and, above all, never becoming a source of embarrassment to British officials. To all intents and purposes, it was a deportation, and one that placed her and her fellow travellers in great danger, as they were travelling to the Gulf of Pechili, into Chinese waters, on a Japanese steamer, which could easily become a target. In the overwhelming heat, dressed in a heavy tweed travelling suit, she felt exhausted and shabby. The experience had a lasting effect on her and how she felt about the poor.

After receiving assistance from the consul in Chefoo, she returned to the Japanese steamer, *Higo Maru*, which sailed on to Newchwang in Manchuria, China. She was received there with great kindness by the British consul and his wife, Mr and Mrs Lowndes Bullock:

"I was not then in circumstances to go to Japan, and after a pleasant week at the dreariest and kindliest of ports, I took a 'Bean Boat' for the week's voyage to Muk-den, my friends not realising what the result would be of five days and nights of incessant rain. The forthcoming day the rain began again, and we were soon entangled in the torrents and currents of the vast inundation eight feet deep, which has turned the magnificent plain of eastern Manchuria into a malarious inland sea. I saw the destruction of over 30 prosperous villages, and had the happiness of saving some lives. But the storm of wind and rain and the darkness were terrific. I was ill, and lay on my camp bed for three days in soaked bedding and clothing, the mat roof of the junk letting in the rain everywhere, and I was so weak when we reached the landing for Muk-den that I was lifted into the cart. I have suffered ever since from the effects of malaria and exposure to chill. Just within sight of the house of Dr Ross at Muk-den, the cart over turned, and with the shaft mule rolled down a declivity and I onto the roof and broke my right arm which after being in splints and a sling for six weeks, emerged usable though weak. With this my misfortunes ended."[10]

The plains of eastern Manchuria endured extremes of heat and cold, and were prone to flooding. Inland roads were almost non-existent, and when it rained after periods of drought, they turned to rivers of mud. It was easier to travel in winter when the ground was frozen hard or by the low-draft bean boats in the summer. Malaria had been rare in Manchuria until the flood of 1888, when water levels rose by 20 feet on the plains, leaving ponds and marshland as they receded, the ideal conditions for malaria epidemics, which occurred frequently in the following years.[11]

Breaking her right arm was disastrous, as she had begun writing the manuscript for her book on Korea. But she greatly impressed staff at the mission hospital with her energy and bravery, learning to write with her left hand when she was suffering from such ill health.[12]

She did make a remarkable recovery, and the enforced period of recuperation provided an opportunity to explore Mukden, which was regarded as the second city of the Chinese empire, gaining 'a good deal of the inner life and opinion of the upper i.e. official class.' This unique view of the culture and people was gained through the connections of the mission hospital run by Dr Christie and Dr Ross, both of whom had studied and adhered to the etiquette of Chinese customs. They were fluent Chinese speakers, and had gained the respect and support of the local community. They had also secured donations from local mandarins and officials, which helped fund the hospital.

A major donor was General Tso, commander of the Chinese forces in Manchuria. His philanthropy, behaviour and self-sacrifice greatly impressed Isabella.[13] The experience provided her with a close-up view of the political tensions of the area and an insight into how unintentional discourteous actions by Europeans caused great offence to the local population. This would inform and influence her travels in China, leading to her adopting Chinese dress, since tight-fitting tailored clothes were considered unseemly and offensive, even for men; a short jacket and fitted trousers were considered highly inappropriate, even discourteous.[14]

At home, press coverage of the political situation in China, Japan and Korea was accompanied by a small story, which appears to have originated from *The Scotsman*, entitled 'An English Lady Among the Coreans'. This described Isabella as the best known of the British nationals in the region. From the *Coventry Evening Telegraph* to the *Western Gazette*,[15] this short story was reprinted, giving some indication of her fame and possibly the concern for her safety at the time.

The sinking by the Japanese of the *Kowshing*, a troopship carrying 1,200 Chinese, and subsequent actions in Korea, triggered the declaration of war on 1st August.[16]

Prior to this, Mukden was tolerant of foreigners; though they might have been referred to as devils,

The Royal Cake or The Western Empires sharing China between them. Left to right: Queen Victoria (1819–1901), Kaiser Wilhelm II (1859–1941), Tsar Nicholas II (1868–1918), Marianne, symbol of the French Repuplic, and Mutsuhito (1852–1912), Emperor of Japan, from *Le Petit Journal*, 16th January, 1898, colour lithograph by Henri Meyer.

this name was prefixed with 'honourable'. This situation changed rapidly as Chinese troops en route to Korea marched through Mukden at the rate of 1,000 a day. After a stay of six weeks, Isabella escaped just in time:

"I left at a time when it was regarded as a great risk to go the three miles to the river, but was quite unmolested and reached Newchwang after a most pleasant trip, not knowing that I escaped by one hour from the outbreak of piracy and murder in which my boat was one of those marked for attack."[17]

From Newchwang, Isabella travelled to Peking via Chefoo and Tientsin. To her delight, at Chefoo she was reunited with her luggage and the money that she had left behind in Seoul.[18] In Tientsin, she gave at least three talks, one to Chinese women in the native chapel via an interpreter called Mr King, another to fifty missionaries and a third to the Tientsin Literary Society on Ladak, Balte and Western Tibet. The *North China Herald* and *Supreme Court & Consular Gazette* reported the lecture under the heading 'A Distinguished Traveller':

"Mrs. Bishop's books are very popular in Tientsin and a large and friendly audience assembled to hear her. The lecture embodied all the literary charm so constantly evident in her books."[19]

Perhaps not so pleased to see her was the British consul in Peking, who was concerned about the worsening situation:

"I came up here, somewhat, or rather much against the wish of the English minister and consul, who only gave me the pass because they said I had won a reputation for being 'the most prudent of travellers'! In the five days in a solitary house boat on the Peiho and on the canal from thence here, I met with nothing perilous or disagreeable, and for a fortnight I have gone about freely here on foot and on a mule cart, with only my faithful Chinese

servant, without encountering hostility or rudeness anywhere, even though I have taken many photographs with my tripod camera."[20]

Isabella used the British Legation in Peking as a base and an address from which to send a journal letter to John Scott Keltie (secretary of the Royal Geographical Society), giving an account of her experiences in Korea and China. Abruptly, however, on 5th October, Sir Robert Hart, inspector general of the Chinese Imperial Maritime Customs Service, ordered all married customs officers to southern stations, and all European women and children to leave Peking. The Chinese Army had been defeated in a major battle at Phyong-yang, Korea, on 15th September and huge losses had been incurred by the Chinese at sea, inflicted by the Japanese. The fear in Peking was that the population would rise against all foreigners and a massacre would take place. Isabella had no choice but to leave, but not before sending a letter to *The Times*, assuring readers that 'in the opinion of several old and well informed residents Peking has never been so safe.'[21] That evening, she also gave a lecture to the Oriental Society of Peking, honouring a commitment to speak after being elected an honorary member:

"… in the glorious Hall of the Dragons in this legation to an audience consisting of the whole diplomatic leaders, the officers of the Chinese customs, and the professors in the Imperial College, and never found people kinder or more sympathetic."[22]

This showed Isabella's steely courage and determination to do her duty, and remain calm in the face of mounting panic and fear. It marked the end of her travels in China in 1894.

She longed to return to Korea, but instead embarked on a steamer bound for Vladivostok, partly on the advice of her doctors, who recommended a colder climate to ease the symptoms of malarial fever. After spending only a month in

Russia, however, she returned to Nagasaki, Japan, and formed a plan to visit missions in China. In 1895, she made a brief visit to Korea, to stay with Sir Walter Hillier, the British representative in Seoul, but it was still impossible for her to travel extensively in Korea because of the war. The tour of missions provided an alternative.

It may have been her experience in Mukden that changed Isabella's previously rather low opinion of missionaries and their work. As she freely admitted in 1899, during her early travels in Asia, she gave 'mission stations a wide berth'[23] and was not 'an enthusiast regarding foreign missions', but she spent her time in China in 1895 staying with them and devoted two chapters in *The Yangtze Valley and Beyond* to the Hangchow Medical Mission Hospital and the Protestant missions in China.

She greatly admired the work undertaken by the hospital and the high professional standards of the attached medical school. As it was part funded by mission societies, she wanted to explain the work that was carried out (over 14,000 new patients annually) so that donors at home would understand and continue to support it. She was more critical of the work of missionaries, stressing the need to study the language carefully, and to gain an understanding of Chinese etiquette and social customs. She was most critical of the amount of time taken in leave, 'on furlough', or 'incapacitated for work by maternal duties'. However, at the end of the chapter, she added a conciliatory note (see display quote).

Since many missions were based in ports along the coast, she travelled in reasonable comfort by

"Having ventured on the criticisms and suggestions, I must add that much of the wisest, most loving, most self-denying, and most successful work that I saw done in China was done by women."[24]

steamer or houseboat. She began her journey at Hong Kong, where she was met by 'a gathering of Missionaries – Muirheads, Moules, Pruens, Mrs Stewart, Mrs Wedderburn'.[25] She passed from one mission to another, her first stop being Swatow followed by Amoy, Foochow and on to Shanghai. Then she took a boat down to Hangchow, exploring Shao-Hsing and Ningpo before spending a week on the Chusan Archipelago. Much of this period was spent in very agreeable exploration and travel, staying as a house guest, being treated as something of a celebrity and photographing with relative ease. At the end of May, she wrote to her publisher:

"I have now been travelling in China for three months with great satisfaction and interest, and have got about a hundred photographs as a record of my journey. I have travelled quite alone, and have not met with anything disagreeable. I am just going to Japan for the summer, to go through a course of blisters for my spine, which I hurt considerably, more than three months ago. I have a project of some very serious travelling in the late autumn and winter if these remedies are successful."[26]

The damage to her spine had been caused in 1895, when she had been thrown from a rickshaw that overturned. Reading between the lines, however, it would appear that she had been born with a form of curvature of the spine: in a letter to Mrs Blackie, she mentions her deformed spine.[27] She was also short in stature. Her spine was her nemesis: whenever she was in an accident, it would

Isabella's boat, "a small house-boat of about twenty tons, flat bottomed, with one tall mast and big sail, a projecting rudder, and a steering sweep on the bow". Her 'passenger accommodation' consisted of "a cabin the width of the boat, with a removable front, opening on the bow deck, where the sixteen boatmen rowed, smoked, ate and slept round a central well in which a preternaturally industrious cook washed bowls, prepared food, cooked it, and apportioned it all day long, using a briquette fire."

always be her spine that seemed to cause the most serious pain (in 1850, when she was eighteen, she had undergone an operation to remove a fibrous tumour).[28] The treatment in Japan appears to have been a great success, and she spent her time visiting the thermal springs, writing and working on her photography.

Isabella did not return to start "some very serious travel" in China until January, 1896. In the intervening months, she had returned to Korea (a peace treaty had been signed by China and Japan on 17th April, 1895) and travelled in the northwest of the country, including visiting the ravaged city of Phyong-yang and the site of the battle where her friend, General Tso, had died. During this time, she continued to work on her Korean book and perfect her photography. At the beginning of January, 1896, Isabella was in Shanghai, writing a report on her progress to John Murray IV, as she prepared to make her way to northwestern Szechuan.

"I have written some chapters on Korea and am taking my notes with me proposing to continue writing while tied up at nights on the Upper Yangtze."[29]

In Shanghai, she engaged Be-dien as a servant/ interpreter. He was willing to face the possible risks and hardships of the journey. At the time, travelling in

China was difficult because of the lack of roads and anti-foreigner sentiment. She was also proposing to travel in very remote and uncharted areas. A Chinese interpreter would need to be very resourceful and resilient. She purchased locally-made travelling trunks and baskets, including an open bamboo armchair in which to be carried. The plan was to travel as far as possible by the Yangtze river and then continue on foot, with Isabella being carried in the chair.

The travelling chair was something of a problem. There was a strict etiquette for how a woman should get in and out of one, and it was improper for a woman to travel in an open chair, regardless of age or status. Isabella acknowledged that the open chair caused much of the trouble, but how was she to record the landscape she travelled through if she could not see it? The open chair was more of an issue in China than a woman travelling on her own, which at times appears to have appalled her fellow countrymen. Traveller and archaeologist Sir Austen Henry Layard wrote to Hallam Murray, John Murray III's second son:

"No one who has heard the howl of an enraged Chinese mob can ever forget it, it is an echo of a bottomless pit."

"I must say I think the woman must be devoid of all delicacy and modesty who could travel as she did, without a female attendant, among a crowd of dirty Persian muleteers and others. Had there been an imperative act of duty or some precise end in view it might have been different, but as far as I can gather she had no object but to satisfy her curiosity and love of travel."[30]

A characteristic of Isabella's writing style was to document the commerce and industry of the places she passed through. At the Yangtze port of Hankow, for example, she recorded the Russian merchants dominating the production of 'brick tea', describing their factories and management of the trade with steamers of the Russian Volunteer Fleet; the Germans with their albumen factories; the tonnage of shipping entering the port; and the amount of kerosene oil imported from Russia, America and Sumatra (16,055,000 gallons in 1898). As well as informing her readers, she was making it clear just how much foreign influence already existed on the Yangtze, part of the subtext of her book, *The Yangtze and Beyond*. Facts would be checked, verified and, if necessary, updated on her return, giving the text a more current feel.

The Yangtze river would shape the first part of the journey, and its seasonal rise and fall fascinated her:

"The annual rise and fall of the Great River can be counted on with tolerable certainty … from forty feet or thereabouts at Hankow to ninety feet and upwards at Chungking. During three months of the year the rush of the vast volume of water is so tremendous that traffic is mainly suspended, and even in early June many hundreds of junks are laid up until the autumn in quiet reaches between Chungking and Wan Hsien."[31]

Leaving in January made it possible to ascend the river as far as Wan Hsien. She travelled by steamer as far as Ichang, and from there by a small houseboat, navigating the many rapids with the help of trackers. As well as being damp and cold, sometimes too cold to sleep, it was dangerous and challenging. Before ascending rapids, the passengers would disembark and scramble over the bolder-strewn shore. It took seventy trackers to haul her boat up the Hsin-tan rapids with fraying ropes, drums and gongs beating time, with the river adding to the deafening clamour as it rushed through the gorge.

Mr Stevenson and Mr Hicks of the China Inland Mission with Be-dien, Isabella's interpreter. Stevenson and Hicks accompanied her as far as Wan Hsien, where they procured a boat for her onward journey. She had engaged Be-dien in Shanghai: "a tall, very fine-looking, superior man … who abominated 'pidgun,' spoke very fairly correct English, and increased his vocabulary daily during the journey. He was proud and had a bad temper, but served me faithfully, was never out of hearing of my whistle except by permission, showed great pluck, never grumbled when circumstances were adverse, and never deserted me in difficulties or even perils."

At Wan Hsien, three chair bearers and four porters were engaged via a *hong* (a transport manager) to take Isabella to Paoning Fu, a journey of seventeen days. The overnight halts were somewhat trying: basic rooms, sometimes swarming with vermin, off a stable yard, shared with animals. Even so, she managed to summon up her nerve to eat many a hearty meal, slept well and came to enjoy what at first had seemed a hopeless situation:

"The tripod of my camera served for a candle stand, and on it I hung my clothes and boots at night, out of the way of rats. With these arrangements I successfully defied the legions of vermin which infest Korean and Chinese inns, and have not a solitary tale to tell of broken rest and general misery. With absolute security from vermin, all else can be cheerfully endured."[32]

Overnight halts were a problem because of the stir created by her arrival. This could range from curiosity to extreme hostility – from holes drilled through the walls of her room followed by whispering and giggling, to a full-blown riot with shouts of 'Foreign devil!', 'Child eater!', 'Beat her!', 'Kill her!', 'Burn her!' At Liang-shan, barricaded in her room, she sat with her revolver, ready to fire, until a mandarin sent soldiers to break up the riot and protect her.[33]

Distrust of foreigners and anti-foreign feeling in general were widespread. European global expansion and interference in 19th-century China had resulted in wars and lesser conflicts. The Taiping Rebellion (1850–64), a civil war that resulted in the deaths of approximately 20 million civilians and soldiers, had its roots in the spread of Christianity; its leader, Hing Xiuquan, believed he was the younger brother of Jesus Christ.[34] The Opium Wars, and subsequent imposition of trade agreements and expansion of treaty ports open to foreign trade led to the establishment of foreign settlements, with their interests and alien ways, in prominent positions in many Chinese cities.

At Paoning Fu, Isabella broke her journey, staying in the Ladies' Mission House of the China Inland Mission before making her way, via Kuan Hsien, to Chengtu Fu. It was on her journey to Kuan Hsien that she was knocked unconscious by a volley of stones. The effects of the attack remained with her for over a year. She took some time at Kuan Hsien to recover. After this, she did have an escort, but the experience marked her, as illustrated in a letter to John Murray IV:

"The real draw back however was the hostility of people which grew week by week and made travelling unpleasant as well as dangerous … No one who has heard the howl of an enraged Chinese mob can ever forget it, it is an echo of a bottomless pit."[35]

It took three months to reach Chengtu Fu, where Isabella decided to follow the River Min into the mountains. As she journeyed north, she enjoyed the changing landscape, describing it as the "Grandest Scenery I ever saw, Switzerland and Kashmir rolled into one." She was also met with polite friendliness. She was travelling on a trade route, the Sung-pan Ting road, which crossed a major route into Tibet, the road to Mou-Kung Ting, and so she met caravans of mules carrying wool and medicinal roots. She encountered rope bridges linking gorges, while the houses had thick sloping walls to withstand the wind. This route took

"… for days the Great River hurried us remorselessly along. There was no time to take in anything. A pagoda or a city scarcely appeared before it vanished."

her as far as Somo, before circumstances forced her to turn south.

On the return journey, her party was caught in a severe snowstorm, which lasted two days. Much to her surprise, however, she found the route out of the mountains to be more gloriously beautiful than the way in, with intense colours and scents. Passing through the heat of the Chengtu Plain to Chengtu Fu, she hired a flat-bottomed *wupan* to begin the 2,000-mile river journey back to Shanghai. She set off on 20th May, and with the Yangtze still rising, it took approximately five weeks to reach the port:

"… past temples, pagodas and grey cities on heights; past villages gleaming white midst dense greenery; past hill, valley, woodland, garden cultivation. And signs of industry and prosperity; past junks laid up for the summer in quiet reaches, and junks with frantic crews straining like ourselves; and still for days the Great River hurried us remorselessly along. There was no time to take in anything. A pagoda or a city scarcely appeared before it vanished." [36]

Isabella returned to Shanghai in June, to discover that it was the wrong time to make the arduous journey home. Having been advised to avoid all exertion, she decided to spend the hot summer months in a mountain resort in Japan, where she could rest and work on her Korea book. This brought to a conclusion her 8,000 miles of journeying in China.

It was only after returning home that she was encouraged by friends to write about China, to share the unique perspective she had gained in the three years of her travels.

During Isabella's time in China, a war had been fought and lost, and foreign powers had increased their influence in the country, with Russia, France and Germany intervening after the war to force Japan to return the Liaodong peninsular to China. [37] A secret alliance was concluded by Russia and China. As she described it, 'The Dragon Throne reeled and righted itself.' [38]

The Yangtze Valley and Beyond, the book Isabella's friends had urged her to write, is quite different in tone and style to her earlier publications. It was dedicated to the Marquess of Salisbury, the Prime Minister, and her concluding remarks clearly set out her views on the state of China at the time. Her admiration for the country and its people shines through, and she leaves no doubt that China was not 'in decay' and that its 'industry, thrift, resourcefulness and complete organization of both labour and commerce, meet the traveller at every turn.' One reviewer of the book described it as 'one of the most thoroughly documented accounts of late nineteenth century China ever written.'

Not bad for an account of a journey 'undertaken for recreation and interest solely' or 'but to satisfy her curiosity and love of travel.' [39]

Mrs Bishop in Manchu dress.

THE AUTHOR IN MANCHU DRESS

1894

In 1894, Isabella experienced a series of disasters while travelling that had a profound effect on her understanding of China and its people.

Deported from Korea, and without money or luggage, Isabella was forced to travel to China where she experienced a flood on the Manchuria Plain. During the deluge, her boat rescued drowning villagers amid terrific storms. She succumbed to malaria, and then, within sight of her destination, the city of Mukden, she was injured when the cart in which she was travelling overturned, breaking her arm.

As a result of these misfortunes, she was compelled to spend two months recovering, during which she was introduced to the culture and people of Mukden by the missionary doctors, who were fluent in the local language. This gave her a unique opportunity to gain an understanding of the political situation, and of how people lived and viewed the Europeans among them. Later she travelled to Peking, but it was her time in Mukden that had the greatest effect on how she viewed China and its people in the future.

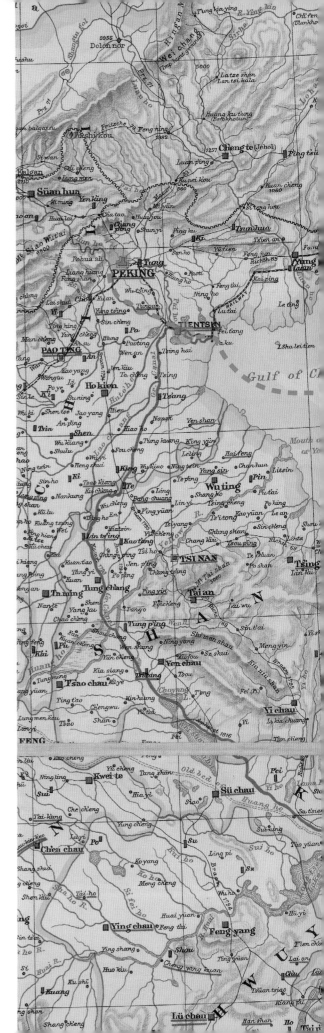

Temple at Chefoo, belonging to Li Hong Chang

Isabella landed at Chefoo, a treaty port, in June, 1894, without money, luggage, passport
or letters of introduction. In desperation and with much reluctance, she turned to the British
Embassy and was surprised by the kindness displayed by the consul, Clement Allen.

*"I needed no proof of identity or anything else, he only desired to know what he could do for me.
My anxiety was not quite over, for I had to make the humiliating confession that I needed money,
and immediately he took me to Messrs. Ferguson and Co., who transact banking business, and
asked them to let me have as much as I wanted. An invitation to tiffin followed…"*

1894

Gelatin silver print

10.8 x 14.9cm

Text from *Korea and Her Neighbours*, Volume 1, by Mrs Bishop (Isabella L. Bird) FRGS

Mandarin's Palace, Newchwang

This photograph is recorded as the Mandarin's Palace. Included in the view at the right-hand side, perhaps unintentionally, is the bow of a steamer in the treaty port of Newchwang.

"This dreary, solitary-looking place of mud and muddy water, was the great trade-port of one of the most prosperous provinces of the empire. The British Consul and his wife, Mr and Mrs Lowndes Bullock, gave her [Isabella Bird] a warm and reassuring reception, and she stayed with them till July 4…"

1894
Gelatin silver print
11.2 x 15.8cm
Text from *The Life of Isabella Bird (Mrs Bishop)*, by Anna M. Stoddart

The Gate of Victory, Mukden

Mukden was a walled city with eight deeply arched great gateways with iron-studded doors. In 1894 they were still closed at night, preventing travellers from entering or leaving the city after dusk.

*"Muk-den, the capital of Manchuria,
is officially the second city of the Empire.
In it are duplicated all the official boards,
save one, that exist in Peking, the capital
of the Empire. Thus Muk-den possesses
its Board of Rites and Ceremonies,
of Punishments, etc. etc., just like Peking.
Close to Muk-den are the ancestral graves
of the Manchu dynasty."*

1894

Gelatin silver print

11.2 x 15.8cm

Text from *Chinese Pictures: Notes on Photographs Made in China*, by Mrs J.F. Bishop FRGS

The Temple of the God of Literature at Mukden

"In every province of the Empire the God of Literature stands highest in the Chinese Pantheon, and it is interesting to note that the God of War stands low, though in China, as in other countries, we know women are devoted to his worship. In no country of the world does literature stand in such high estimation: by means of it the poorest man may climb to the highest post in the Empire. Nothing so helps a man to a career as a knowledge of the literature of his country. Reverence for it has become a superstition, and societies exist for collecting waste paper and saving any writing from indignity by burning it in furnaces erected for the purpose in every town."

1894

Gelatin silver print

14.4 x 10.8cm

Text from *Chinese Pictures: Notes on Photographs Made in China*, by Mrs J.F. Bishop FRGS

The Temple of the Fox, Mukden

"Another temple at Muk-den, greatly frequented by mandarins. A group of them is seated in the centre. The temple is situated close to the city wall, which is shown in process of decay, the descending roots of the trees stripping off its facing, which lies and will continue to lie on the ground. It is an admirable illustration of the way things are allowed to go to ruin in China. The Chinese will undertake new works; they seldom repair old ones, and an aspect of decay is consequently frequently visible."

1894

Gelatin silver print

10.6 x 15.5cm

Text from *Chinese Pictures: Notes on Photographs Made in China*, by Mrs J.F. Bishop FRGS

Passenger cart at Mukden

"*A typical mode of conveyance in Manchuria the Northern Province. The arrangement for carrying luggage is seen at the back of the cart. It is very similar to the Legation state carriage in construction, being entirely without springs. It is only possible to use such a conveyance in such a roadless country, with any security from broken bones, by adopting the precaution to pad the whole of the interior, bottom, top, and sides with thick mattresses. In the course of a journey of three miles only, Mrs. Bishop had the misfortune to be thrown into the top of the cart in an upset with such violence that her arm was broken and her head severely cut. In her case, unfortunately, the top of the cart was not padded.*"

1894

Gelatin silver print

11.1 x 15.9cm

Text from *Chinese Pictures: Notes on Photographs Made in China*, by Mrs J.F. Bishop FRGS

Temple students

Although recorded as 'Temple students', this group is more likely to be medical students with Dr Dugald Christie (centre, back) at Mukden Mission Hospital. The doctor's hat can be seen on the right of the picture.

"The Mission Hospital is one of the largest and best equipped in the Far East, and besides doing a great medical and surgical work, is a medical school in which students pass through."

1894

Gelatin silver print

10.6 x 14.9cm

Text from *Korea and Her Neighbours*, Volume 1, by Mrs Bishop (Isabella L. Bird)

Patients at Mukden Mission Hospital

"For over five weeks she [Isabella] remained in Moukden, taking a deep interest in our work and in all that happened, visiting the hospital constantly, inquiring into the history of each patient, and taking photographs. We were greatly impressed by her energy and keenness in the face of ill-health and suffering. Her right arm being disabled she immediately set herself to learn to write with her left hand, and in this way part of the manuscript of her book on Korea was written."

1894

Gelatin silver print

10.9 x 14.3cm

Text from *Thirty Years in Moukden, 1883–1913, Being the Experiences and Recollections of Dugald Christie, C.M.G.*

The entrance to the British Legation, Peking

"The Legation is a fine old palace, which formerly belonged to a member of the Imperial Family. The photograph shows the entrance to the first courtyard. The Legation compound is very extensive, and contains several courtyards with buildings round each. It is very highly decorated, the designs shown in this picture being elaborately wrought in lacquered work of gold and colours. This is the building recently attacked by the Chinese in their attempt to destroy all foreigners, including the members of the various European Legations who took refuge with Sir Claude Macdonald."

1894

Gelatin silver print

11.1 x 15.1cm

Text from *Chinese Pictures: Notes on Photographs Made in China*, by Mrs J.F. Bishop FRGS

The state carriage of the British Legation, Peking

Standing on the left is Mr Campbell, British Majesty's Consular Service; sitting is Mr Beauclerk, first secretary of the Legation; Mr Grant Duff, second secretary, is on the right.

"There are practically no carriage roads in China, so that there is virtually no carriage traffic. This rough, springless cart is the only carriage drawn by animals at the disposal of the Legation."

1894

Gelatin silver print

10.8 x 15.2cm

Text from *Chinese Pictures: Notes on Photographs Made in China*, by Mrs J.F. Bishop FRGS and 'Snap-shots in the Far East' from *World Wide Magazine*, 1898.

Entrance to the College of the Student Interpreters, Peking

"Student interpreters are young Englishmen who enter the College to prepare themselves for the Consular Service. At eighteen they have to pass their entrance examination. They receive given posts in connection with one of the various Chinese Consulates. All our Chinese Consuls are drawn from this College. It stands within the grounds of the Legation, which is the building shown on the right of the picture."

1894

Gelatin silver print

10.5 x 14.9cm

Text from *Chinese Pictures: Notes on Photographs Made in China*, by Mrs J.F. Bishop FRGS

Private entrance to the Imperial Palace, Peking

"A subject of considerable interest, owing to the mystery surrounding the members of the Imperial Family. The photograph was taken from the wall of the Purple or Forbidden City, in which only the Imperial Family and their entourage have the right to dwell. The building in the centre, which is roofed with yellow tiles, is supposed to be the residence of the Emperor, but where he does actually reside remains a mystery. The entrance to the Palace is through the arches in the building on the left."

1894

Gelatin silver print

10.8 x 15cm

Text from *Chinese Pictures: Notes on Photographs Made in China*, by Mrs J.F. Bishop FRGS

Hsi Chih Men gate, Peking

"Perhaps the most interesting and picturesque feature of the country is its city gates. There is a great family likeness between them, the usual fort-like building surmounting the wall where it is pierced by the gate. It is not a fort, however. In it are kept the gongs and other musical instruments by means of which are announced the rising and the setting of the sun. This is the gate which was blown up by the Japanese in their recent attack on the entry into the city. It is the largest and most important gate in Peking."

1894

Gelatin silver print

10.3 x 15cm

Text from *Chinese Pictures: Notes on Photographs Made in China*, by Mrs J.F. Bishop FRGS

Bronze armillary, Peking Observatory

Dating from the Ming Dynasty, the armillary is cast in bronze and shows the most beautiful example of artistry and workmanship.

"The stand of this piece of mechanism has a mythological significance, and its design is of remarkable artistic excellence. Four of the dragons, which play such an important part in Chinese geomancy, are there seen chained to the earth, and upholding the spheres. The perfect modelling and solidity of the metal proves that the art of casting was well understood in those days."

1894
Gelatin silver print
10.8 x 14.7cm
Text from *Illustrations of China and Its People*, by John Thomson

Fort on the wall of Peking

Isabella explored Peking with her faithful Chinese servant and took photographs with her tripod camera of subjects such as the impressive forts on the walls of the city.

"This fort is filled with carronades, old guns still kept there, though absolutely useless, being honeycombed with disuse and rust."

1894

Gelatin silver print

11.1 x 15.3cm

Text from *Chinese Pictures: Notes on Photographs Made in China*, by Mrs J.F. Bishop FRGS

On the wall of Peking

Isabella based herself at the British Legation during her stay in Peking. She did not particularly like Peking, describing *"An atmosphere of decay which broods over the city."*

1894

Gelatin silver print

11.3 x 15.2cm

Text from *Korea and Her Neighbours*, Volume 1, by Mrs Bishop (Isabella L. Bird)

1895

Of all of the periods Isabella spent in China, 1895 was perhaps the year when she had the most leisure and enjoyment, staying as the guest of missionaries as she travelled up the eastern coast.

As well as carrying out a survey of missions, she visited many locations photographed by her mentor, John Thomson. She often set up her camera in similar positions, trying to capture the same viewpoints, continually striving to improve her photographic skills and develop her artistic compositions.

Isabella was continually surprised by the glorious beauty of the Chinese spring; the lakes with their deep wooded bays, inlets and perfect shores all mirrored in silver waters. The ancient cities of Hangchow and Shao-Hsing fascinated her with their culture, temples and shrines.

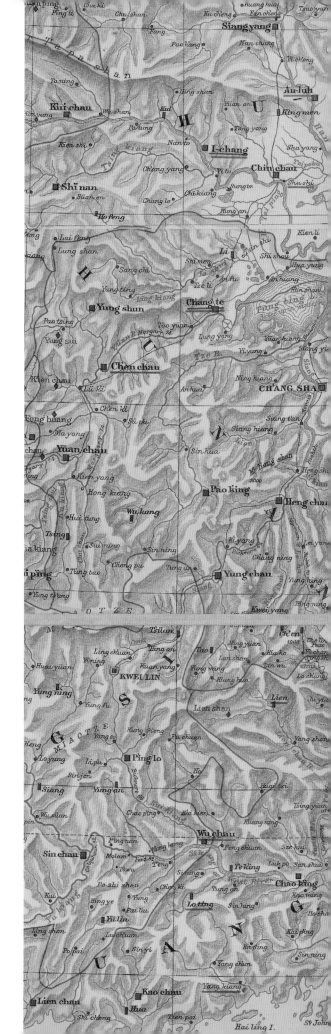

A street depopulated by the plague in Hong Kong

Isabella arrived in Hong Kong by steamer on 27th February, 1895 in the middle of an outbreak of Bubonic plague. It raged through the poorer districts, causing 8,600 deaths between 1894 and 1901. Many people left the city during the outbreak and the photograph records the deserted streets. Isabella stayed with the bishop of Hong Kong, Bishop John Shaw Burdon and his wife Phoebe, using the bishop's palace as her base.

1895
Gelatin silver print
15.1 x 10.8cm
Text from *The Life of Isabella Bird (Mrs Bishop)*, by Anna M. Stoddart

Hoisting mast on Isabella's boat, *Veronica*, at Swatow

This type of boat was used for visitation work in the countryside around Swatow by the Protestant Mission. Making a photographic record of what she saw was an important element of Isabella's tour of missions.

"She bore credentials, therefore, to the four great Protestant missions in China – the Church Missionary Society, the London Missionary Society, the China Inland Mission, and the Presbyterian Mission."

1895

Gelatin silver print

10.3 x 15cm

Text from *The Life of Isabella Bird (Mrs Bishop)*, by Anna M. Stoddart

"The hospitals of England and China have evidently many things in common. Inside the compound of the English Presbyterian Medical Mission of Swatow, the patients buy their bottles of the vendor as if they were patients of Guy's or St. Bartholomew's. A similar incident is to be witnessed in Smithfield any day of the week. It may be mentioned that the hospital of this particular Medical Mission is nearly the largest in the East. In times of stress it accommodates four hundred patients, and in the proportion of its cures is one of the most successful in the world."

Bottle seller and hospital patient

1895
Gelatin silver print
15.2 x 10.7cm
Text from *Chinese Pictures: Notes on Photographs Made in China*, by Mrs J.F. Bishop FRGS

Missionaries in Chinese dress

"It is not only improper but scandalous for a woman to be seen in a tight bodice, or any other fashion which shows her figure, and a foreign girl lays herself open to remarks which I scarcely think she would like to hear, when she appears in a fly-away hat, bent up and bent down, on which birds, insects, feathers, grasses, and flowers have been dumped down indiscriminately! The Mission Board of one large and successful Mission has found it desirable to issue rules for missionaries regarding dress and etiquette, and the China Inland Mission everywhere, and the Church Missionary Society missionaries in Sze Chuan have solved the difficulty by adopting Chinese costume, the only Oriental dress which Europeans can wear with seemliness and dignity."

1895

Gelatin silver print

11.2 x 15.2cm

Text from *The Yangtze Valley and Beyond*, by Mrs J.F. Bishop (Isabella L. Bird), FRGS

Mission building, Swatow

In 1895, Isabella wrote, *"I liked and admired the English Presbyterians at Swatow and Wuking far more than any body of men and women that I have seen. In the Fukien Province a great deal of work is being done, but the most spiritual part by the fifty missionaries of the C.M.S."*

1895
Gelatin silver print
10.5 x 14.5cm
Text from *The Life of Isabella Bird (Mrs Bishop)*, by Anna M. Stoddart

European children and Chinese servants, Fukien

The children are sitting on a wheelbarrow that has a large central wheel and normally would be used for transporting produce. The small bound foot of the Chinese woman sitting behind is just visible.

"… a girl with unbound feet would have no chance of marriage, and a bridegroom finding that his bride had large feet when he expected small ones, would be abundantly justified by public opinion in returning her at once to her parents."

1895

Gelatin silver print

10.8 x 15cm

Text from *The Yangtze Valley and Beyond*, by Mrs J.F. Bishop (Isabella L. Bird), FRGS

Madame Poo-Foo

There is no information on the subject of this portrait, Madame Poo-Foo, but time was taken to improvise a studio setting by draping a cloth to create a backdrop.

Gelatin silver print

15.8 x 11.1cm

A farmhouse in Fukien, southern China

"An illustration of the Patriarchal system. When a son marries and brings home his wife, he literally brings her home – that is, to his father's house; but a new gable is added to those in existence, and the house increased for the accommodation of the new family; a custom which has its counterpart in Italy and other parts of Europe to-day."

1895

Gelatin silver print

10.6 x 15.1cm

Text from *Chinese Pictures: Notes on Photographs Made in China*, by Mrs J.F. Bishop FRGS

Ficus religiosa, Fukien

"A kind of banyan tree found in every village of the South and South Central Provinces of China. Its foliage covers an enormous extent of ground. The tree itself is an object of worship, and an altar for the burning of incense is always found beneath it."

1895

Gelatin silver print

10.7 x 14.7cm

Text from *Chinese Pictures: Notes on Photographs Made in China*, by Mrs J.F. Bishop FRGS

Presbyterian mission buildings, Wuking Fu

Isabella estimated that *"two thousand four hundred and fifty-eight Protestant workers (including wives) represent the missionary energies and the many divisions of Christendom."*

1895

Gelatin silver print

10.4 x 15.2cm

Text from *The Yangtze Valley and Beyond*, by Mrs J.F. Bishop (Isabella L. Bird), FRGS

The mode of sepulchre in Fukien, and throughout southern China

"A horseshoe-shaped excavation is made in a hillside facing south, the whole construction being faced with stone. There is in this mode of arranging graves a similarity to that adopted by the Etruscans."

1895

Gelatin silver print

10.7 x 15.1cm

Text from *Chinese Pictures: Notes on Photographs Made in China,* by Mrs J.F. Bishop FRGS

Junks at Foochow

"The usual destination of such junks is one of the ports on the China coast, or at furthest, Siam, Java, Borneo, or the straits of Malacca. At their moorings, these huge, clumsy vessels seem like mid-stream dwelling-places, fastened down by solid foundations to the river's bed, but when full rigged for sea, they look well, and even at times make good sailing before the wind; indeed in every way they are more manageable than appearances would betoken."

1895

Gelatin silver print

10.6 x 15cm

Text from *Illustrations of China and Its People*, Volume II, by John Thomson

Cobbler at Foochow

"A very important personage in China. He deals, however, with men's shoes only. The women wear tiny satin or brocaded things which they mostly make and mend themselves. They are from two to three inches long, and with hard-working women in the fields the feet never extend four inches ... The binding process begins very early—between four and five generally, though sometimes it is postponed to a later date, when the process is much more painful. The four toes are doubled under the foot, and the large toe folded on the top. When bound together a sort of club-foot or hoof results, but the women manage to walk in spite of their deformity."

1895

Gelatin silver print

10.6 x 15.1cm

Text from *Chinese Pictures: Notes on Photographs Made in China*, by Mrs J.F. Bishop FRGS

A baby tower, Foochow

"When a baby dies, and the parents are too poor to give it a decent burial, they drop its poor little body into one of the openings in this tower. A Guild of Benevolence charges itself with the task of clearing out the tower every two or three days, burying the bodies with all religious rites and ceremony."

1895
Gelatin silver print
14.7 x 10.6cm
Text from *The Yangtze Valley and Beyond*, by Mrs J.F. Bishop (Isabella L. Bird), FRGS

The Altar of Heaven

The area around Foochow City was noted for its great beauty and spectacular scenery. The use of figures in this composition may have been chosen to give a sense of scale.

"A fine picture of an open-air altar outside Foochow City."

1895

Gelatin silver print

10.5 x 14.8cm

Text from *Chinese Pictures: Notes on Photographs Made in China*, by Mrs J.F. Bishop FRGS

River port

"Monster liners under their own steam at times nearly fill up the channel, their officers yelling frantically at the small craft which recklessly cross their bows; great white, two-storeyed paddle arks from Ningpo and Hankow, local steamers, steam launches owned by the great firms, junks of all builds and sizes, manageable by their huge rudders, sampans, hooded boats, and native boats of all descriptions, lighters, and a shoal of nondescript craft make navigation tedious, if not perilous, while sirens and steam whistles sound continually."

1895

Gelatin silver print

11.2 x 15.6cm

Text from *The Yangtze Valley and Beyond*, by Mrs J.F. Bishop (Isabella L. Bird), FRGS

The Zig-Zag Bridge and tea house, Shanghai

This picture shows a view of spectators on the bridge, watching as Isabella takes the photograph. She was escorted by Mr Fox of HM Consular Service when she explored Shanghai beyond the foreign settlement.

"… as a foreign woman is an every-day sight in the near neighbourhood, the people minded their own business and not mine, and I was even able to photograph without being overborne by the curious."

1895

Gelatin silver print

11.2 x 15.8cm

Text from *The Yangtze Valley and Beyond*, by Mrs J.F. Bishop (Isabella L. Bird), FRGS

Municipal Temple, Shanghai

"The buildings and fantastic well-kept pleasure grounds of the Ching-hwang Miao, which may be called the Municipal Temple..."

Although not confirmed, the European man perched on the fence is most likely Isabella's guide, Mr Fox of HM Consular Service. Later he became Consul-General of Peking.

1895

Gelatin silver print

10.4 x 15cm

Text from *The Yangtze Valley and Beyond*, by Mrs J.F. Bishop (Isabella L. Bird), FRGS

West gate, Hangchow

"One of the friendliest cities to the foreigner. The cry of 'Foreign devil!' is never heard within its walls. The people have had time to learn how much they profit by the trade the foreigner brings, and by the efforts of the missionaries to ameliorate the condition of the very poor by their hospitals. Hangchow is a great centre of the silk trade. The whole city, which has a population of 700,000, and the principal street of which is five miles long, is surrounded by a wall faced with hewn stone, such as is shown in the photograph. It is pierced by many gates. It is a treaty port, two days' journey from the great foreign settlement of Shanghai."

1895

Gelatin silver print

10.2 x 14.1cm

Text from *Chinese Pictures: Notes on Photographs Made in China*, by Mrs J.F. Bishop FRGS

Ancient pagoda, Hangchow

"The situation of Hangchow is beautiful, separated only by a belt of clean sand from the bright waters of the Ch'ieng T'ang river. The south-western portion is built on a hill, from which broad gleams of the sea are visible; and to the west, just outside the walls, is the Si Hu [Western Lake], famous throughout China, a lovely sheet of water, surrounded by attractive country houses, temples and shrines, studded with wooded islands connected by ancient and noble causeways..."

1895

Gelatin silver print

15.2 x 11cm

Text from *The Yangtze Valley and Beyond*, by Mrs J.F. Bishop (Isabella L. Bird), FRGS

The librarian of the Ting Library, Hangchow

"Hangchow is a great centre of Chinese culture and literature. It possesses the Ting Library, the finest private library in China, appropriately housed in buildings adjoining the 'palace' of the Ting family. The arrangements for the storage and classification of books are admirable, and a very gentlemanly and intelligent son of the enlightened possessor is the enthusiastic and capable librarian. The treasures of this library are open freely to anyone who introduces himself by a card from an official."

1895

Gelatin silver print

15.2 x 10.4cm

Text from *The Yangtze Valley and Beyond*, by Mrs J.F. Bishop (Isabella L. Bird), FRGS

Wen Lan Ge, the Imperial Library, Hangchow

"... the islands themselves crowned with decorative pavilions, some of which are Imperial, and are surrounded by the perfection of Chinese gardening, as in the case of the beautiful Imperial Library, with its ferneries, rockeries, quaint ponds, and flowering shrubs."

The reference to the islands refers to the islands of the Western Lake and Hangchow.

1895

Gelatin silver print

10.8 x 15.4cm

Text from *The Yangtze Valley and Beyond*, by Mrs J.F. Bishop (Isabella L. Bird), FRGS

God of Thunder, Ling Yin Temple

*"The temples and shrines of this beautiful glen are visited daily by crowds from Hangchow,
and have such a reputation for sanctity and efficacy as to attract 100,000 pilgrims annually.
The dell is guarded by two colossal figures, under canopies, the gods of Wind and Thunder,
very fine specimens of vigorous wood carving, and by an antique pagoda."*

1895
Gelatin silver print
15.9 x 11.2cm
Text from *The Yangtze Valley and Beyond*, by Mrs J.F. Bishop (Isabella L. Bird), FRGS

The Temple of the Five Hundred Disciples of Buddha, Hangchow

"Near the lake is a deep, long dell, the cliffs of which are recessed for stone images, and which contains several famous temples, one the temple of the 'Five Hundred Disciples,' who, larger than life-size, adorn its spacious corridors."

1895

Gelatin silver print

10.8 x 15.4cm

Text from *The Yangtze Valley and Beyond*, by Mrs J.F. Bishop (Isabella L. Bird), FRGS

Fashionable tea house, Hangchow

"Hangchow impresses one with a general sense of well-being. I did not see one beggar. The people are well clothed and fed, and I understood that except during epidemics there is no abject poverty. It is a grand centre for the trade of a hundred cities, and much of the tea and silk sold in Shanghai and Ningpo passes through it."

1895

Gelatin silver print

10.8 x 15.4cm

Text from *The Yangtze Valley and Beyond*, by Mrs J.F. Bishop (Isabella L. Bird), FRGS

Yue Fei Temple, Hangchow

The temple was built in honour of Yue Fei,
a general of the Southern Song dynasty,
who fought against the Jurchen Jin dynasty
during the Jin–Song wars, after the capital of
China was moved south to Hangchow.
The temple dates from 1221 and has been
restored several times since that date.

1895
Gelatin silver print
10.8 x 15.2cm

89

Church Mission Society Hospital, Hangchow

"The men's and women's hospitals, of which the illustration only shows portions, are of the latest and most approved European type. They are abreast of our best hospitals in lighting, ventilation, general sanitation, arrangement and organisation, and the facility of obtaining the celebrated Ningpo varnish, really a lacquer, which slowly sets with a very hard surface, reflecting much light and bearing a weekly rub with kerosine oil, greatly aids the sanitation."

1895

Gelatin silver print

10.5 x 15.2cm

Text from *The Yangtze Valley and Beyond*, by Mrs J.F. Bishop (Isabella L. Bird), FRGS

Three leper women, Hangchow Leper Hospital

"Of the patients treated in Hangchow last year one thousand were in-patients. 'Discharged cured' might be written against the great majority of their names, and those who were incurable were greatly benefited, as in the case of the lepers, whose 'grievous wounds' are closed and healed, and whose pains are subdued."

1895

Gelatin silver print

15.4 x 11cm

Text from *The Yangtze Valley and Beyond*, by Mrs J.F. Bishop (Isabella L. Bird), FRGS

Patients, Hangchow Hospital

"Crowds of out-patients marshalled like an army, carefully trained assistants knowing and doing their duty, catechists, ward assistants, cashiers, photographers, cooks, gardeners, artisans, make up the crowd which in all the morning hours swarms over the staircases of the hospital and round the great entrance."

1895

Gelatin silver print

10.9 x 15.3cm

Text from *The Yangtze Valley and Beyond*, by Mrs J.F. Bishop
(Isabella L. Bird), FRGS

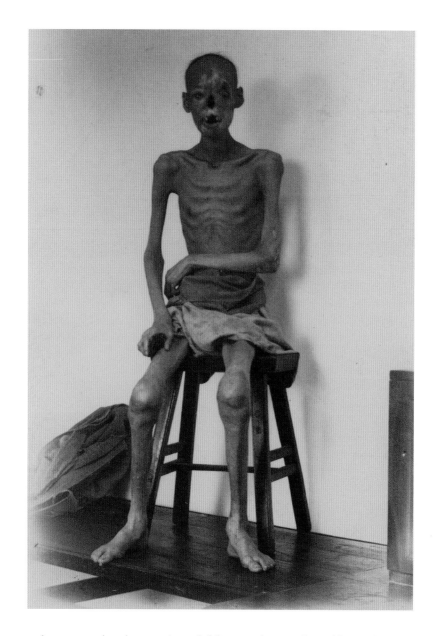

Leper and opium eater of 20 years' standing, Hangchow

"The opium habit is regarded as a disease, for the cure of which many smokers voluntarily place themselves in opium refuges at some expense, and at a great cost of suffering, and in the market towns, thronged with native traders, there is to be seen on many stalls among innumerable native drugs and commodities, a package labelled 'Remedy for Foreign Smoke,' 'foreign smoke' being the usual name for opium in Western China."

1895

Gelatin silver print

14.5 x 9.8cm

Text from *The Yangtze Valley and Beyond*, by Mrs J.F. Bishop (Isabella L. Bird), FRGS

The gate of a Forbidden city

"Though only two miles from a treaty port, it is believed that no foreigner has ever had the foolhardiness to enter this gate. It is a city of the fifth order only; but such is the hatred and detestation in which the foreigner is held, it would be almost certain death to him to enter it. This hatred of the foreigner is a very curious characteristic of the country. No one can tell how it has arisen, for though one can understand that the attempts of Western nations to force open the ports of the country, and the seizure of territory by certain of them, and perhaps the advent of the missionaries, are causes enough to provoke opposition and hatred, they do not account for its ferocity."

1895

Gelatin silver print

10.4 x 14.1cm

Text from *Chinese Pictures: Notes on Photographs Made in China*, by Mrs J.F. Bishop FRGS

Three-sided theatre stage at a temple

Theatre stages were often constructed as part of a temple. These ancient and historic theatres have great cultural significance and vary greatly in design with the oldest being single storey structures. In 1896, during her journey in the Yangtze Valley and beyond Isabella caused great offence in the town of Paoning Fu by setting up her camera and tripod on a theatre stage.

1895

Gelatin silver print

10.9 x 15.4cm

Approach to ancient temple, Shao-Hsing

"Her visit to me was very interesting, in every way. I introduced to her notice some new features of interest daily, and her stock of photographic plates soon came to an end in her endeavour to secure lasting pictures of the ancient buildings and monuments with which our city abounds." Reverend W. Gilbert Walshe.

1895

Gelatin silver print

10.8 x 15.2cm

Text from *The Life of Isabella Bird (Mrs Bishop)*, by Anna M. Stoddart

Ancient temple at Shao-Hsing

Shao-Hsing enthralled Isabella, who originally intended to stay only one night and eventually remained there almost one week. The architecture and history of the city fascinated her.

1895

Gelatin silver print

10.8 x 15.3cm

Temple of Confucius, Shao-Hsing

"Wherever there is a magistrate there is a temple to Confucius, in which the magistrates do homage in memory of the Great Teacher."

The grey band along the bottom of the image is believed to have occurred when Isabella was toning or enamelling the print.

1895

Gelatin silver print

10.4 x 15.4cm

Text from *Chinese Pictures: Notes on Photographs Made in China*, by Mrs J.F. Bishop FRGS

The Emperor Yu at Temple Yu, Shao-Hsing

"… even in the face of the largest and noisiest crowds, Mrs Bishop proceeded with her photography and her observations as calmly as if she were inspecting some of the Chinese exhibits in the British Museum."

1895
Gelatin silver print
15.8 x 11.2cm
Text from *The Life of Isabella Bird (Mrs Bishop)*, by Anna M. Stoddart

Pagoda at Shao-Hsing

Pagodas were built to fulfil a religious function and were often part of a temple complex. They are thought to have originated in India. The pagoda at Shao-Hsing has a finial.

1895

Gelatin silver print

10.7 x 15.2cm

Text from *The Life of Isabella Bird (Mrs Bishop)*, by Anna M Stoddart

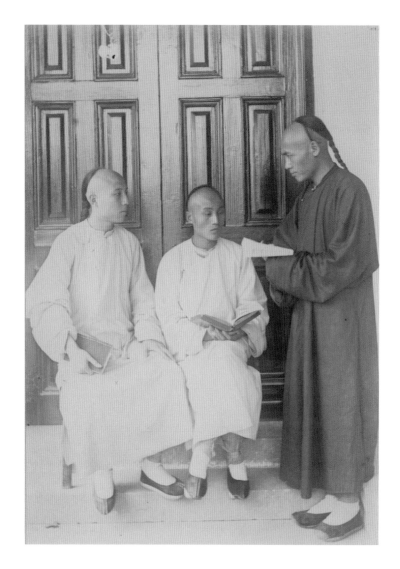

Three Christian students, Ningpo

Charles Joseph Hoare was a priest for the Church Mission Society in Ningpo and founded a training college for Chinese evangelists.

"Isabella believed that if the nations of the East are to be evangelised it must be by native agents, she was immensely interested in Mr. Hoare's splendid work of training young men as catechists, and perhaps eventually clergymen."

1895

Gelatin silver print

14.9 x 10.5cm

Text from *The Life of Isabella Bird (Mrs Bishop)*, by Anna M. Stoddart

Granite pillars, Tien-how-kung Temple of the Fukien Guild, Ningpo

"Chinese carving in stone has much merit, even in such an intractable material as granite. The depth and sharpness of the cutting and the undercutting are remarkable, and the absolute realism." [1]

"The Fukien Temple was originally founded during the twelfth century. It was at different times destroyed and rebuilt, and was finally raised to its present magnificent proportions about the beginning of the eighteenth century." [2]

1895

Gelatin silver print

14.8 x 10.9cm

Text from [1] *The Yangtze Valley and Beyond*, by Mrs J.F. Bishop (Isabella L. Bird), FRGS, and [2] *Illustrations of China and Its People*, Volume III, by John Thomson

The Hall of the Four Heavenly Kings at Tien-dong Monastery, near Ningpo

Ningpo was reached by travelling *"through a region of great fertility, prosperity, and beauty."* The monastery is south west of Ningpo in the wooded mountains. Ningpo is one of China's oldest cities, a trading city on the silk road and a major port.

1895

Gelatin silver print

10.8 x 15.2cm

Text from *The Life of Isabella Bird (Mrs Bishop),* by Anna M. Stoddart

Incremation urns of Buddhist priests, Tien-dong Monastery, Ningpo

The Tien-dong Monastery of the Heavenly Child, near Ningpo, is a famous Chan (Zen)
Buddhist temple. It is believed to date back to around 300 AD.

1895
Gelatin silver print
10.7 x 15.5cm

Temple pavilion in Puto, Chusan Archipelago

"At Ningpo the commissioner of Customs kindly lent me the Customs tender, a fast-sailing lorcha, for a week, and engaging a servant, I visited the Chusan Archipelago in glorious weather, spending three days on the remarkable island of Putu, the Island of Priests, sacred to Kwan Yin, the goddess of mercy, and two at Tinghai, on the island of Chusan..."

1895

Gelatin silver print

11 x 15.4cm

Text from *The Yangtze Valley and Beyond*, by Mrs J.F. Bishop (Isabella L. Bird), FRGS

The thousand-armed Kwan yin with attendants

Kwan yin, the Goddess of Mercy, was sacred to the Buddhist island priests of Puto. The island is one of the larger in the Chusan Archipelago and is a place of great beauty and sacred importance.

1895

Gelatin silver print

15.7 x 11.1cm

Divinities at a temple in Puto

"Temples were for the first time erected on this island as early as 550 A.D. The revenues for the support of these various religious establishments are derived from three sources: the rent of church lands, the contributions of pilgrims, and the labours of the mendicant priests."

1895

Gelatin silver print

10.6 x 15.2cm

Text from *Illustrations of China and Its People*, Volume III, by John Thomson

Fishing fleet, Tinghai, Chusan Archipelago

During the first opium war in 1840, the British occupied the Chusan Archipelago. Isabella spent two days at Tinghai.

"… at Tinghai, on the island of Chusan, where the graves of the four hundred British soldiers who died there during our occupation present a melancholy spectacle of neglect and disrepair."

1895

Gelatin silver print

11 x 15cm

Text from *The Yangtze Valley and Beyond*, by Mrs J.F. Bishop (Isabella L. Bird), FRGS

1896

This was the year of Isabella's great journey up the Yangtze and beyond, the exploration that would cause her much personal hardship.

Isabella's journey introduced her to the very varied culture and life of the Chinese people, the country's magnificent productive fertile plains and epic sweeping landscapes. The rise and fall of the mighty Yangtze made her aware of the power and scale of the country, which fascinated her the more she travelled in it.

Her adventures and exploration left her with a passion for China and the Chinese and above all a deep, enduring respect for the resourcefulness and energy of its inhabitants.

ISABELLA BIRD

Hankow from Han Yang

"Enormous quantities of goods are everywhere waiting for transit, for Hankow is the greatest distributing centre in China, and the big steamers lying at the bund, or at anchor in the stream, and the thousand junks which crowd the waterways, seem barely sufficient for her gigantic commerce."

1896

Gelatin silver print

10.7 x 14.8cm

Text from *The Yangtze Valley and Beyond*, by Mrs J.F. Bishop (Isabella L. Bird), FRGS

Members of the police force, Hankow

"… a mixed force of Europeans, Sikhs, and Chinese preserves order and security in the settlement by day and night."

1896

Gelatin silver print

11 x 15.5cm

Text from *The Yangtze Valley and Beyond*, by Mrs J.F. Bishop (Isabella L. Bird), FRGS

ISABELLA BIRD

Wadded winter clothing

"The wadded winter clothing is made in autumn and worn without change until spring, though the better off and more particular wear inner garments which are washed regularly."

1896

Gelatin silver print

11.2 x 15.7cm

Text from *Thirty years in Moukden, 1883–1913, Being the Experiences and Recollections of Dugald Christie, C.M.G.*

Isabella's boat prepared for departure

*"The weather was raw, grim, and sunless. I
had had a fire day and night in my room at
the customs, and a fireless, draughty boat
was a shivery prospect, but things usually
turn out far better than either prophecies
or expectations, and this voyage was no
exception."*

1896

Gelatin silver print

10.2 x 15.2cm

Text from *The Yangtze Valley and Beyond*, by Mrs J.F. Bishop
(Isabella L. Bird), FRGS

Nan-to, Yangtze river

"The night at Lao-min-tze was too cold for sleep, and before dawn I heard the wild chant of the boatmen as great cargo boats, with fifty to ninety rowers, swept down the stream. We untied at daylight, and, after passing the lovely village and valley of Nan-to, admired and wondered all day."

1896

Gelatin silver print

11 x 15.2cm

Text from *The Yangtze Valley and Beyond,* by Mrs J.F. Bishop (Isabella L. Bird), FRGS

Bed of the Yangtze in winter, Ta-tan rapid

"A friend lately asked me if I whiled away the time by 'walking on the river banks,' thinking, doubtless, of the level towing paths of the meadows of the Thames and Ouse. The accompanying illustration shows the banks of the Yangtze below Wan Hsien at their best, and the pleasant possibilities for strolling! The river-bed, there forty feet below its summer level, is an area of heaped, contorted rock-fragments, sharp-edged, through which one or more swirling streams or violent rapids pursue their course, the volume of water, even at that season, being tremendous."

1896

Gelatin silver print

11.2 x 15.7cm

Text from *The Yangtze Valley and Beyond*, by Mrs J.F. Bishop (Isabella L. Bird), FRGS

Ping-shu gorge, Hsin-tan

"... a stretch of deep, calm water in peaceful contrast – the Ping-shu gorge."

1896

Gelatin silver print

11.2 x 15.7cm

Text from *The Yangtze Valley and Beyond*, by Mrs J. F. Bishop (Isabella L. Bird), FRGS

The Hsin-tan rapid on the Yangtze river

"A glorious sight the Hsin-tan is as seen from our point of vantage, half-way up the last cataract, a hill of raging water with a white waterfall at the top, sharp, black rocks pushing their vicious heads through the foam, and above, absolute calm. I never saw such exciting water scenes – the wild rush of the cataract; the great junks hauled up the channel on the north side by 400 men each, hanging trembling in the surges, or, as in one case, from a tow-rope breaking, spinning down the cataract at tremendous speed into frightful perils; whilst others, after a last tremendous effort, entered into the peace of the upper waters."

1896

Gelatin silver print

11.1 x 14.6cm

Text from The Yangtze Valley and Beyond, by Mrs J. F. Bishop (Isabella L. Bird), FRGS

Hsin-tan on the Yangtze

"Hsin-tan is a wild and beautiful village, and has an air of prosperity. Many junk owners have retired there to spend their days, and the comparative cleanliness and good repair are quite striking. One orange-embowered village on a spur has a temple with a pagoda built out over the edge of the cliff, without any obvious support."

1896

Gelatin silver print

10.8 x 14.9cm

Text from *The Yangtze Valley and Beyond*, by Mrs J.F. Bishop (Isabella L. Bird), FRGS

Passage junk

"In passage junks the open space forward is diminished as much as possible, most of the deck being housed over, but in cargo junks less than half is covered.

"We call the junks 'lumbering craft,' but no craft anywhere are more skilfully handled; none run such risks; no crews are better disciplined to act together and at a second's notice in cases of emergency; no men work so desperately hard on such small pay and with such poor food."

1896

Gelatin silver print

10.8 x 14.8cm

Text from *The Yangtze Valley and Beyond*, by Mrs J.F. Bishop (Isabella L. Bird), FRGS

Village on the Yangtze

"A village which might claim to be a town, at a height of fully 400 feet, is not only piled up on terraces, but the houses are built out from the cliff on timbers, and the flights of steps leading from terrace to terrace are so steep that I made no attempt to climb them."

1896

Gelatin silver print

10.8 x 14.9cm

Text from *The Yangtze Valley and Beyond*, by Mrs J.F. Bishop

(Isabella L. Bird), FRGS

The Yangtze above Ichang

"The change from a lake-like stretch, with its light and movement, to a dark and narrow gorge black with the shadows of nearly perpendicular limestone cliffs broken up into buttresses and fantastic towers of curiously splintered and weathered rock…"

1896

Gelatin silver print

10.6 x 15.2cm

Text from *The Yangtze Valley and Beyond*, by Mrs J.F. Bishop (Isabella L. Bird), FRGS

ISABELLA BIRD

Trackers' houses

"Each boat carries enough men to pull her up against the strong stream, but at a rapid she needs many more, and during the navigation season coolies from long distances migrate to the river and put up mat huts as close to it as possible, to which dealers in food, tobacco, samshu, and opium at once gravitate, along with sellers of bamboo tow-ropes. Nor are rough amusements wanting. Rough, dirty, noisy, these temporary settlements are. Their population is from forty or fifty to over 400 men. When the river rises the huts are removed, and the coolies return to other avocations."

1896

Gelatin silver print

11 x 15.3cm

Text from *The Yangtze Valley and Beyond*, by Mrs J.F. Bishop (Isabella L. Bird), FRGS

Isabella's trackers at dinner

"The crews, which in big junks number 120 men, are engaged at Ichang. For the upward voyage, lasting from thirty to fifty days, they get about four shillings and their food, which is three meals a day of rice, with cabbage fried in a liberal supply of grease, and a little fish or pork on rare occasions, and for coming down, which rarely takes more than ten days (I did it in a wupan in a little over four), about eighteenpence and food, and indeed many crews work their passage down for food only. For this pittance these men do the hardest and riskiest work I have seen done in any country, 'inhumanly hard,' as Consul Bourne calls it, week after week, from early dawn to sunset."

1896

Gelatin silver print

10.5 x 15.3cm

Text from *The Yangtze Valley and Beyond*, by Mrs J.F. Bishop (Isabella L. Bird), FRGS

Lukon Gorge

"It was always changing, too. If it were possible to be surfeited with turrets, battlements, and cathedral spires, and to weary of rock phantasies, the work of water, of solitudes and silences, and of the majestic dark green flow of the Great River, there were besides lateral clefts, each with its wall-sided torrent, with an occasional platform green with wheat, on which a brown-roofed village nestled among fruit trees, or a mountain, bisected by a chasm, looking ready to fall into the river, as some have already done, breaking up into piles of huge angular boulders, over which even the goat-footed trackers cannot climb."

1896

Gelatin silver print

14.7 x 10.6cm

Text from *The Yangtze Valley and Beyond*, by Mrs J.F. Bishop (Isabella L. Bird), FRGS

Temple near Kueichow

"The Upper Yangtze is remarkable for the picturesque beauty of its cities at a distance, and their situations, almost invariably on irregular heights, backed by mountains, and with fine gardens and trees within their crenelated stone walls, which follow the contour of the site invariably, with one or more lofty pagodas denoting the approach, and with yamen and temple roofs dominating the mass of houses are very imposing."

1896

Gelatin silver print

10.8 x 15cm

Text from *The Yangtze Valley and Beyond*, by Mrs J.F. Bishop (Isabella L. Bird), FRGS

Trackers' houses on the banks of the Yangtze

"Above Kueichow there is a comparatively open reach with steep hills 1,000 feet high, cultivated in patches to their summits, then tinged with green, small villages with wooded surroundings occurring frequently."

1896
Gelatin silver print
11.2 x 15.8cm
Text from *The Yangtze Valley and Beyond*, by Mrs J.F. Bishop (Isabella L. Bird), FRGS

Settlement on the banks of the Yangtze

"Then, wherever the cliffs are less absolutely perpendicular, there are minute platforms partially sustaining houses with their backs burrowing into the rock, and their fronts extended on beams fixed in the cliff, accessible only by bolts driven into the rock."

1896

Gelatin silver print

10.7 x 14.7cm

Text from *The Yangtze Valley and Beyond*, by Mrs J.F. Bishop (Isabella L. Bird), FRGS

Yangtze river

"So far as I could judge of the Great River between Sui Fu, at the junction of the River of Golden Sand and the Min, and Ichang, leaving out the gorges, there are very few reaches in which rapids, races, and rocky broken water are not to be met with. Indeed, it may be said that there is no tranquil water, and Admiral Ho, the superintendent of police for the Upper Yangtze, is probably not exaggerating when in his official Yangtze Pilot he enumerates about a thousand perils to navigation."

1896

Gelatin silver print

15 x 10.8 cm

Text from *The Yangtze Valley and Beyond*, by Mrs J.F. Bishop (Isabella L. Bird), FRGS

Smoke towers on the Yangtze river

"I climbed a height to look at some queer erections, which are seen at intervals of about three miles, on elevations along the river from Ichang to Chungking, making a goodly show. They are white towers, with a red sun painted on the front of each, and stand five in a row. The boatmen say that they are to mark distances, but, according to better authorities they are yen-tun, or 'smoke towers,' and have served the purpose of giving alarm in unsettled times by fires of dry combustibles within. Apparently they have not been repaired for many years."

1896

Gelatin silver print

14.7 x 10.8cm

Text from *The Yangtze Valley and Beyond*, by Mrs J.F. Bishop (Isabella L. Bird), FRGS

Kuei Fu, upper Yangtze river

"*Kuei Fu is a large city, with a very fine wall and noble gate towers, and imposing roofs of yamens and temples are seen above the battlements. At that time it was very hostile to foreigners, and I made no attempt to enter its stately gates, but walked in the beautiful surroundings...*"

1896

Gelatin silver print

10.7 x 14.6cm

Text from *The Yangtze Valley and Beyond*, by Mrs J.F. Bishop (Isabella L. Bird), FRGS

Porcelain-fronted temple at Kuei Fu on the Yangtze river

"I photographed a suburban temple with a porcelain front, where the priests, as is their wont, were quite polite, but on the way back we were 'rushed' by a crowd of men and boys howling and shouting, and using the term yang-kwei-tze, 'foreign devil,' very freely."

1896

Gelatin silver print

10.7 x 14.7cm

Text from *The Yangtze Valley and Beyond,* by Mrs J.F. Bishop (Isabella L. Bird), FRGS

Typical farmhouse

"In such a fertile and beautiful region the absence of animal life is curious. There is no pasturage, the roads are not made for draught, and the cheerfulness of horses, cattle, and sheep about a farmyard is unknown. Buff dogs, noisy and cowardly, and the hideous water buffalo, which looks like an antediluvian survival and has a singular aversion to foreigners, represent the domestic animals."

1896

Gelatin silver print

11.1 x 15.8cm

Text from *The Yangtze Valley and Beyond*, by Mrs J.F. Bishop (Isabella L. Bird), FRGS

Junks, or riverboats, at Wan Hsien

"Illustrating the enormous traffic on the Yangtze. This fringe of boats, closely packed, extends for two miles along the river bank, and is an evidence of the great trade and prosperity of Wan Hsien."

1896

Gelatin silver print

10.8 x 15.2cm

Text from *Chinese Pictures: Notes on Photographs Made in China*, by Mrs J.F. Bishop FRGS

Guest hall, China Inland Mission House, Wan Hsien

"… a truly beautiful paved inner court, one side a roofed-in open space used as a chapel, the other a lofty and handsome Chinese guest-room, as shown in the illustration, with an open front, and the living rooms of the family. A third side is the women's guest-room, and on the fourth are various rooms. Projecting upper storeys and balconies, all carving and fretwork, latticed and carved window-frames with paper panes, tall pillars, and irregular tiled roofs, make up a striking tout ensemble in the midst of which Mr. and Mrs. Thompson, and three ladies, all in Chinese dress, stood to welcome me."

1896

Gelatin silver print

10.7 x 15.3cm

Text from *The Yangtze Valley and Beyond*, by Mrs J.F. Bishop (Isabella L. Bird), FRGS

China Inland Mission House at Wan Hsien

"The streams of visitors to the beautiful guest-halls never ceased by daylight. Miss Ramsay often received forty women at a time. All Sze Chuan women have bound feet, and all wear trousers very much en évidence, those of the lower class women being wrapped round the ankles and tied, those of the upper class being wide and decorated. They asked hordes of questions about domestic and social matters..."

1896

Gelatin silver print

11 x 15.4cm

Text from *The Yangtze Valley and Beyond*, by Mrs J.F. Bishop (Isabella L. Bird), FRGS

Temple at Wan Hsien

"This back country, in which are few level acres, is exquisitely cultivated, and is crossed in several directions by flagged pathways, carried over ascents and descents by good stairs. These usually lead to lovely villages, built irregularly on torrent sides, among a great variety of useful trees."

1896

Gelatin silver print

10.7 x 15.2cm

Text from *The Yangtze Valley and Beyond*, by Mrs J.F. Bishop (Isabella L. Bird), FRGS

A Chinese burial charity

"The care of the dead is imperative on every Chinese, but poverty steps in, a coffin is an unattainable luxury, and without help a proper interment is impossible. Hence in all cities there are benevolent guilds which supply coffins for those whose relations are too poor to buy them, and bury such in free cemeteries, providing, according to Chinese notions, all the accessories of a respectable funeral, with suitable offerings and the attendance of priests. Human bones which have become exposed from any cause are collected and reburied with suitable dignity, and bodies which have remained for years in coffins above ground waiting for the geomancers to decide on an auspicious day for the funeral, until all the relations are dead and the coffins are falling into decay, are supplied with new ones, and are suitably interred."

1896

Gelatin silver print

10.8 x 15.4 cm

Text from *The Yangtze Valley and Beyond,* by Mrs J.F. Bishop (Isabella L. Bird), FRGS

"Sze Chuan is famous for the number and splendour of what are usually called 'widow's arches,' ... I attempted to photograph it, and the chai-jen made the crowd stand to right and left by a series of vigorous pushes, shouting the whole time, 'In the name of the mandarin.' But the people had too much curiosity to be anything but mobile. These arches, or pai-fangs, are put up frequently in glorification of widows who have remained faithful to the memory of their husbands, and who have devoted themselves to the comfort and interests of their parents-in-law and to good works."

Included in the composition is Isabella's travelling chair.

A pai-fang

1896
Gelatin silver print
14.8 x 11cm
Text from *The Yangtze Valley and Beyond*, by Mrs J.F. Bishop
(Isabella L. Bird), FRGS

*"… the grand pass of Shen-kia-chao
(2,900 feet) lifted us above habitation and
cultivation into a solitary mountain region of
rock, scrub, torrents, and waterfalls. The road
ascends the pass by 1,140 steps on the edge
of a precipice, which is fenced the whole way
by granite uprights two feet high, carrying long
granite rails eight inches square. Two chairs
can pass along the whole length. The pass is
grand and savage. There were brigands on the
road, and it was patrolled by soldiers, small
bodies of whom I met in their stagey uniforms,
armed with lances with long pennons
and short bows and arrows."*

The pass of Shen-kia-chao

1896
Gelatin silver print
15.5 x 11.1cm
Text from *The Yangtze Valley and Beyond,* by Mrs J.F. Bishop (Isabella L. Bird), FRGS

Wayside shrine and pai-fang

"... These erections are finer and more numerous in Sze Chuan than I have seen elsewhere in China. Some villages on a day's journey were approached under six stone portals, remarkable for their dignity and artistic perfection."

This pai-fang is positioned next to a wayside shrine.

1896

Gelatin silver print

11.1 x 15.8cm

Text from *The Yangtze Valley and Beyond*, by Mrs J.F. Bishop (Isabella L. Bird), FRGS

A Chinese 'Chatsworth'

"Passing Sar-pu, a village composed almost entirely of fine temples, and through Chin-tai, where the temples are of great beauty, under many highly decorated pai-fangs, and past some Chinese Chatsworths and Eatons, and large 'brick noggin' farmhouses..."

1896

Gelatin silver print

10.5 x 14.7cm

Text from *The Yangtze Valley and Beyond*, by Mrs J.F. Bishop (Isabella L. Bird), FRGS

Bridge and inn of Shan-rang-sar

"But not sub-tropical was the raw, damp, penetrating wind, which blew half a gale at the top of the pass, and pretty miserable was the inn in the fertile, green, malarious hole to which we made an abrupt descent of 1,500 feet. My stout 'regulation' waterproof, which had withstood the storm and stress of many Asiatic journeys, had given way; the waterproof covers of most of the baggage, torn by rough usage, let the water through; and my cushions were soaked. I had only six inches to spare on either side of my stretcher in the absolutely dark and noxious hole in which I slept. The candle-wicks were wet, spluttered, and went out, and I had to eat in the darkness rendered visible by the inn lamp."

1896

Gelatin silver print

15.1 x 10.5cm

Text from *The Yangtze Valley and Beyond*, by Mrs J.F. Bishop (Isabella L. Bird), FRGS

ISABELLA BIRD

A porcelain temple

"As the country became more open, besides these fortified refuges on rocky heights, which suggest possible peril, while the frequency with which solitary houses occur tells of complete security, there are great solitary temples with porcelain fronts in rich colouring, mandarin's and landowners' houses rivalling some of our renowned English homes in size and stateliness."

1896

Gelatin silver print

10.6 x 15.2cm

Text from *The Yangtze Valley and Beyond*, by Mrs J.F. Bishop (Isabella L. Bird), FRGS

The water buffalo

"The water buffalo ploughs, harrows the rice swamps, turns the grain and oil mills, and does many other useful turns. I never saw him used as a beast of burden. It is hard to become reconciled to the appearance of the great 'water ox,' with his mostly hairless, blackish-grey skin, in places with a pinkish hue, and his flat head, carried level with his uncouth, unwieldy body, his flat nose and curved flat horns, looking altogether like a survival from antediluvian days. Buffaloes are uncertain in their tempers, though usually very docile, and, like their owners, are liable to frenzies of fury when frightened."

1896

Gelatin silver print

7.1 x 10.1cm

Text from *The Yangtze Valley and Beyond*, by Mrs J.F. Bishop (Isabella L. Bird), FRGS

Ordinary covered bridge

"The kind of bridge found on a secondary road in Sze Chuan, constructed of wood roofed in with tiles, after the manner of Switzerland, to protect it from the weather."

1896

Gelatin silver print

10.6 x 15.2cm

Text from *Chinese Pictures: Notes on Photographs Made in China*, by Mrs J.F. Bishop FRGS

A lady's chair

"Out in the country there are practically no roads, as we understand roads. … the almost universal mode of passenger transit is by chairs and bearers. The narrowness of the paths is a source of trouble. When two parties of bearers approach each other, there is much shouting to induce one or other to return and make way; but when both come on, one has to get off, or be pushed off, into the swamp by the sides.

"The bearers are patient, much-enduring people, who do their work thoroughly and without complaining, in the face of mud, and rain, and difficult roads. They will carry a traveller from twenty to twenty-five miles a day. When a lady occupies the chair the curtains are rigidly closed. It would be at risk of her life to travel in an open chair."

This image was used in the *The Yangtze Valley and Beyond*, but was taken by Dr Kinnear.

1896

Gelatin silver print

10.5 x 15cm

Text from *Chinese Pictures: Notes on Photographs Made in China*, by Mrs J.F. Bishop FRGS

"All through the Empire province of Sze Chuan, the western province of the Yangtze Basin, markets are held in the market street, specially reserved for the purpose. On market days the street is crowded by thousands of people, the tea and other shops are overflowing, and the noise and shouts of the bargainers are deafening. The shops are generally owned by farmers in the neighbourhood, who let them for the use of merchants on market day. On other than market days they are like deserted villages. No one is to be seen but the caretaker and his family, who are shown in the photograph with the inevitable dog and pig and buffalo. The building on the right is a temple."

A market place or market street in Sze Chuan

1896

Gelatin silver print

14.7 x 10.2cm

Text from *Chinese Pictures: Notes on Photographs Made in China*, by Mrs J.F. Bishop FRGS

Temple of the God of Literature, Paoning Fu

"Officially, Paoning Fu is an important city, having a Taotai, a prefect, and a hsien, and many of its beautiful 'suburban villas' are the residences of retired and expectant mandarins. Its suburbs are quite charming, and its suburban roads are densely shaded by large mulberry trees and the Aleurites cordata. Farther outside are several fine temples in large grounds, and the public library."

1896

Gelatin silver print

10.8 x 15.2cm

Text from *The Yangtze Valley and Beyond*, by Mrs J.F. Bishop (Isabella L. Bird), FRGS

Chinese Protestant Episcopal Church, Paoning Fu

"The church, or cathedral, of which an illustration is given, was built almost entirely with Chinese money and gifts. It is Chinese in style, the chancel windows are 'glazed' with coloured paper to simulate stained glass, and it is seated for two hundred. The persons represented as standing outside are Bishop Cassels [centre], Mr. Williams [left], *and the Chinese churchwarden [right]. There are both churchwardens and sidesmen."*

1896

Gelatin silver print

10.8 x 15.3cm

Text from *The Yangtze Valley and Beyond*, by Mrs J. F. Bishop (Isabella L. Bird), FRGS

"Dr Cassels, who was one of the pioneers, and formerly well known as an athlete at Cambridge, had recently been consecrated bishop, and came from the splendours of his consecration in Westminster Abbey to take up the old, simple, hardworking life, to wear a queue and Chinese dress, and be simply the 'chief pastor.' The native Christians gave him a cordial reception on his return, and presented him with the hat of a Master of Arts and high boots, which make a very seemly addition to the English episcopal dress, giving it the propriety which is necessary in Chinese eyes…"

The Right Reverend Bishop Cassels, Paoning Fu

1896
Gelatin silver print
15.3 x 10.5cm
Text from *The Yangtze Valley and Beyond*, by Mrs J.F. Bishop (Isabella L. Bird), FRGS

China Inland Mission sanitarium, Sin-tien-tze

"... for a few days at Sin-tien-tze, where the China Inland Mission has obtained a large farmhouse for a sanitarium and centre of country work at a height of 2,870 feet. Paoning is only 1,520. This in Lat. 31° 55', was my farthest point north on my Sze Chuan journey."

1896

Gelatin silver print

11.2 x 15.8cm

Text from *The Yangtze Valley and Beyond*, by Mrs J.F. Bishop (Isabella L. Bird), FRGS

Isabella's arrival at a Chinese inn

*"The coolies were, if possible, cheerier and better than those from whom I had reluctantly
parted, and as they were not opium-smokers they were able to feed themselves well, and
thought nothing of travelling thirty miles a day, at a good pace."*

1896

Gelatin silver print

10.2 x 15.2cm

Text from *The Yangtze Valley and Beyond*, by Mrs J.F. Bishop (Isabella L. Bird), FRGS

A hand mill

"The people were quite disposed to be friendly. On arriving one afternoon at a specially lofty hamlet, having learnt much caution as to the use of my camera, I asked if I might 'make a picture' of a mill worked by blindfolded buffalo-cow, as we had not any such mills in my country, and they were quite willing, and stopped the cow at the exact place I indicated. They were friendly enough to take me to another mill, at which two women grind, turning the upper stone by means of poles working in holes. The Chinese use a great deal of wheat flour; it can be purchased at all markets and large villages, and I never used any other."

1896

Gelatin silver print

10 x 7.7cm

Text from *The Yangtze Valley and Beyond*, by Mrs J.F. Bishop (Isabella L. Bird), FRGS

The Ta-lu

"… the Ta-lu, the great Imperial road from Peking to Chengtu. I travelled along this westwards to Mien-chow. A thousand years ago it must have been a noble work. It is nominally sixteen feet wide, the actual flagged roadway measuring eight feet. The bridges are built solidly of stone. The ascents and descents are made by stone stairs. More than a millennium ago an emperor planted cedars at measured distances on both sides, the beautiful red-stemmed, weeping cedar of the province. Many of these have attained great size, several which I measured being from fourteen to sixteen feet in circumference five feet from the ground, and they actually darken the road."

1896
Gelatin silver print
10.5 x 14.8cm
Text from *The Yangtze Valley and Beyond,* by Mrs J.F. Bishop (Isabella L. Bird), FRGS

Watermill, Chengtu plain

"There are frequent water-mills of a very peculiar construction, said by experts to be the oldest form in the world, the wheel being placed horizontally just above the lower level of the water."

1896

Gelatin silver print

11.2 x 15.7cm

Text from *The Yangtze Valley and Beyond*, by Mrs J.F. Bishop (Isabella L. Bird), FRGS

"There were two services in the guest-hall on Sunday, conducted by Mr. Heywood Horsburgh, the superintendent of the Mission, and several classes for women also, but all in a distracting babel – men playing cards outside the throng, men and women sitting for a few minutes, some laughing scornfully, others talking in loud tones, some lighting their pipes, and a very few really interested. This is not the work which many who go out as missionaries on a wave of enthusiasm expect, but this is what these good people undergo day after day and month after month."

The Reverend J. Heywood Horsburgh in travelling dress

1896
Gelatin silver print
14.7 x 10.7cm
Text from *The Yangtze Valley and Beyond*, by Mrs J.F. Bishop (Isabella L. Bird), FRGS

Bridge at Mien-chuh

"After two pleasant days' journey we reached Mien-chuh Hsien a town of 50,000 people, according to the statement of the magistrate's secretary. It is not a handsome town, but it has a beautiful modern bridge over a branch of the Fou, of six stone arches, a fine roof, iron balustrades, and a central roofed tower. It is a busy and prosperous city, with many fine temples and grand mountain views."

1896

Gelatin silver print

10.2 x 14.9cm

Text from *The Yangtze Valley and Beyond*, by Mrs J.F. Bishop (Isabella L. Bird), FRGS

The Erh-wang temple, Kuan Hsien

"The temple left on my journey an impression of beauty and majesty, which nature and art have combined to produce. Outside, glorious trees in whose dense leafage the lesser architectural beauties lose themselves, gurgling waters, flowering shrubs with heavy odours floating on the damp, still air, elaborately carved pinnacles and figures on the roofs, even the screens in front of the doors decorated with elaborate tracery…"

1896

Gelatin silver print

10.5 x 14.9cm

Text from *The Yangtze Valley and Beyond*, by Mrs J.F. Bishop (Isabella L. Bird), FRGS

The roof of the temple, Kuan Hsien

"… while the beauty of the interior is past description: columns of highly polished black lacquer, a roof, a perfect marvel of carving and lacquer, all available space occupied with honorary tablets, the gift of past viceroys, while the shrines are literally ablaze with gorgeously coloured lacquer and painting, and the banners presented by the emperors wave in front."

1896

Gelatin silver print

11 x 15.3cm

Text from *The Yangtze Valley and Beyond*, by Mrs J.F. Bishop (Isabella L. Bird), FRGS

Wine carriers

"The mode of carrying oil and wine in wicker baskets lined with oiled paper of extraordinary toughness, which is much used everywhere. The oil is obtained from various 'oil seeds,' the tough paper by macerating bamboo. Beneath the basket will be noticed a long cylinder. This is the coolie's purse, in which he carries his 'cash,' the small copper or brass coin of the country, which is of such small value that nine pounds weight of copper cash is only worth one English shilling."

1896

Lantern slide

Text from *Chinese Pictures: Notes on Photographs Made in China,* by Mrs J.F. Bishop FRGS

ISABELLA BIRD

Divinity in Wen-shu-yuan temple, Chengtu

"In the entrance portico, tho idol photographed as an illustration recalled me to the tact that China is a stronghold of idolatry. On the other side the divinity looks like a douce, respectable English squire of the days of George III."

1896

Gelatin silver print

15.3 x 11.2cm

Text from *The Yangtze Valley and Beyond*, by Mrs J.F. Bishop (Isabella L. Bird), FRGS

Barrow traffic, Chengtu plain

"These 'machines,' with a big wooden wheel placed so near the centre of gravity as to throw the weight of the load as little as possible on the driver's shoulders, carry goods on platforms on either side and behind the wheel, which is solid. One man can propel five hundredweight. Heavy loads have one man to propel and another to drag them. They move in long files, their not altogether unmelodious creak being heard afar off, and the stone road is deeply grooved by their incessant passage."

1896

Gelatin silver print

10.6 x 14.6cm

Text from *The Yangtze Valley and Beyond*, by Mrs J.F. Bishop (Isabella L. Bird), FRGS

Entrance to grounds of city temple, Kuan Hsien

"We left Kuan by the west gate, near a very fine temple, to which the picturesque mass of lacquered pillars and roofs in the illustration is only the outer entrance."

1896

Gelatin silver print

10.7 x 14.7cm

Text from *The Yangtze Valley and Beyond*, by Mrs J.F. Bishop (Isabella L. Bird), FRGS

Double-roofed bridge

"The whole of the first fortnight's journey was along the deep, wild gorge of the greater or lesser Min. It differs widely from ordinary Chinese travelling, and has a strong resemblance to the wild gorges of the Yangtze. The mountains rise from the river to a height of over 3000 feet. Ghastly snow-cones look over them, their slopes, always steep, often break up into cliffs 400 or 500 feet high; the river has often not a yard of margin, and hurries along, crashing and booming, a thing of purposeless power and fury, which has never been tamed of mankind, its sea-green colouring a thing of beauty, and its crests and stretches of foam white as the snows which give it birth."

1896

Lantern slide

Text from *The Yangtze Valley and Beyond*, by Mrs J.F. Bishop (Isabella L. Bird), FRGS

Kan-chi

"I cannot attempt to convey to the reader any idea of the glories and surprises of that long day's journey. It was a perfect extravagance of grandeur of form and beauty of colouring, and the sky approached that of Central Asia in the brilliancy of its bright pure blue. Every outline was sharp, but the gorges were filled with a deep blue or purple atmosphere; the sunlight was intense. All are built of stone, all look more or less like fortifications, all have flat roofs, and most have brown wood rooms or galleries, much decorated with rude fretwork, supported on carved beams projecting from their upper storeys."

1896

Gelatin silver print

14.2 x 10.3cm

Text from *The Yangtze Valley and Beyond*, by Mrs J.F. Bishop (Isabella L. Bird), FRGS

Rock temple, Li-fan Ting

*"This small, grey city, on whose expansion Nature places her veto, looks the final outpost of
Chinese civilisation – the end of all things. A well-built, narrow, crenelated wall runs between
Li-fan Ting and the river, hems it in, and then in a most fantastic way climbs the crests of two
mountain spurs, which wall in a ravine behind the town, bare and rocky as all else is, looking like
great flights of uncannily steep stairs, following the steep and irregular contour of the ground. It
has a remarkable yamen, which, lacking space for lateral expansion, has developed skywards;
a temple on a rock, brilliantly coloured; and a fine temple in the narrow street, rich in effective
wood-carving, and possessing a huge bas-relief of the Dragon."*

1896

Gelatin silver print

15.2 x 10.7cm

Text from *The Yangtze Valley and Beyond*, by Mrs J.F. Bishop (Isabella L. Bird), FRGS

Village of Wei-gua

"Four hours after leaving Li-fan we halted at the large village of Wei-gua, with a very large lama-serai, said to contain two hundred lamas, cresting the rock above it, and a fine castle in a dominant position. The illustration gives the lower and un-picturesque fragment of the village grouped round the remains of a large square tower."

1896

Gelatin silver print

11 x 14.7cm

Text from *The Yangtze Valley and Beyond*, by Mrs J.F. Bishop (Isabella L. Bird), FRGS

"A marked feature of this stretch of the Siao Ho is the extraordinarily abrupt bends which it makes, and that at most of these a sugar-loaf peak, forest clothed below, and naked rock above rises sheer from the river-bed, possibly to a height of from 2,000 to 3,000 feet. Great openings allow of inspiring views of high, conical, snow-clothed peaks, heavily timbered below the snow."

A sugar-loaf mountain, Siao Ho

1896

Gelatin silver print

15.4 x 10.6cm

Text from *The Yangtze Valley and Beyond*, by Mrs J.F. Bishop (Isabella L. Bird), FRGS

Bridle track by the Siao Ho

"On the left the mountains descend to the torrent in a series of precipices. On the right a space, averaging twenty yards in width, gives room for the bridle-path and for a perfect glory of vegetation. From this rise forest-clothed precipices and peaks as on the other side. Between them thunders the small river, narrower but much fuller in volume than below, green with a greenness I have never seen before or since, and white with foam like unto driven snow, booming downwards with a fall of over sixty feet to the mile, its brilliant waters hasting to lose themselves 2,000 miles away in the turbid Yellow Sea."

1896

Gelatin silver print

10.5 x 14.5cm

Text from *The Yangtze Valley and Beyond*, by Mrs J.F. Bishop (Isabella L. Bird), FRGS

ISABELLA BIRD

Castle at Chu-ti

"A Man-tze official escort was at once provided, consisting not of armed and stalwart tribesmen, but of two handsome laughing girls, full of fun, who plied the distaff as they enlivened our way to Chu-ti. Nor was this fascinating escort a sham. Before starting each of the girls put on an extra petticoat. If molestation had been seriously threatened, after protesting and calling on all present to witness the deed, they would have taken off the additional garments, laying them solemnly (if such laughing maidens could be solemn) on the ground, there to remain till the outrage had been either atoned for or forgiven, the nearest man in authority being bound to punish the offender."

1896

Gelatin silver print

14.7 x 10.7cm

Text from *The Yangtze Valley and Beyond*, by Mrs J.F. Bishop (Isabella L. Bird), FRGS

Chinese officer and spearmen, Mia-ko

Concern over robbers in the area prompted the local headman to provide an escort for Isabella's safety.

"We left Matang early in May, accompanied by the Chinese officer, who had wisely remained in the Hang-Kia valley, and ten stalwart spearmen from Mia-ko. I started on foot accompanied by this escort, leaving the others to follow at their leisure; some of the baggage being on yaks, which having been as usual lost on the mountain, caused considerable delay. When our force was mustered it numbered twenty-five men. Two of the wild-looking tribesmen rode big yaks, monstrous in their winter coats; all were armed with lances, and short, broad-bladed swords, and a few carried long and much-decorated matchlock guns. Of course we saw nothing of the bandits, and when we had passed their beat the spearmen quietly disappeared, apparently ignorant of their right to baksheesh. The ghastly, grinning head of a third bandit hung in a cage in the village."

1896

Gelatin silver print

10.6 x 14.9cm

Text from *The Yangtze Valley and Beyond*, by Mrs J.F. Bishop (Isabella L. Bird), FRGS

Lama-serai and headman's house, Mia-ko

"After we crossed to the right bank of the dwindling river a great number of Man-tze men and women met us, and escorted us up steep stony slopes to the large village of Mia-ko, with its many-storeyed houses, a feudal castle, and a lama-serai like an ugly factory, with 150 monks. We were received in the house of the T'ou-jen, the father of our muleteer, who has a patriarchal household of married sons and daughters with their children, and farms on a large scale."

1896

Gelatin silver print

11.2 x 15.8cm

Text from *The Yangtze Valley and Beyond*, by Mrs J.F. Bishop (Isabella L. Bird), FRGS

Village of Rong-kia

"After an ascent, and a halt at an extraordinary village of square towers, from each of which a single, brown wood room projected at the top, another steep ascent took us to the top of a spur, from which we looked down on the valley of the Rong-kia below its junction with the other streams, there a broad, swift river, free from rapids and cataracts, and bridged in several places."

1896

Lantern slide

Text from *The Yangtze Valley and Beyond*, by Mrs J.F. Bishop (Isabella L. Bird), FRGS

"The first view of it sleeping in the soft sunshine of a May noon was one never to be forgotten. The valley is fully one mile wide, and nine miles long, and snow peaks apparently close its western extremity. All along the 'Silver Water,' there were wheat fields in the vivid green of spring; above were alpine lawns over which were sprinkled clumps of pine and birch, gradually thickening into forests, which clothed the skirts of mountains, snow-crested, and broken up here and there into pinnacles of naked rock."

Approach to Somo

1896

Lantern slide

Text from *The Yangtze Valley and Beyond*, by Mrs J.F. Bishop (Isabella L. Bird), FRGS

Somo castle

"Somo castle, on its eastern side, is a most striking building, built into the rock of the spur on which it stands. It has a number of windows with decorative stone mullions, the lowest over twenty feet from the ground. Its many roofs are planted thick with prayer-flags, and projecting rooms and balconies of brown wood, with lattice-work fronts, hang from its eastern side over the precipice."

1896

Gelatin silver print

10.7 x 15.7cm

Text from *The Yangtze Valley and Beyond*, by Mrs J.F. Bishop (Isabella L. Bird), FRGS

Somo castle yard

"The castle yard is spacious and singularly clean; the entrance is handsome, and is faced by a huge dragon, boldly and skilfully painted on a plastered stone screen. Poles with crowns from which yak's tails depend, and the trident, as in Western Tibet, surmount the entrance. The whole is most substantially built of stone, and I looked in vain for any trace of decay or disrepair. The altitude is about 7,518 feet."

1896

Gelatin silver print

10.4 x 15.4cm

Text from *The Yangtze Valley and Beyond*, by Mrs J.F. Bishop (Isabella L. Bird), FRGS

A Heshui family, Ku-erh-Kio

"At Ku-erh-Kio, where after a journey of eleven hours I sat nearly two hours among dogs, pigs, and fowls, waiting for the people to return from the mountain and give us shelter, I slept for the last time on a roof under the stars, the earliest sight in the morning being glories of light and shade, of forest, cataract, and mountain, and the sparkle of a peak reddening in the sunrise, like unto the Matterhorn, which the people called Ja-ra (king of mountains)."

From Ku-erh-Kio, Isabella made her descent to Kuan and the Chengtu, where she joined the River Min, beginning a 2,000-mile river journey that would take her back to Shanghai.

1896

Gelatin silver print

11.2 x 15.7cm

Text from *The Yangtze Valley and Beyond*, by Mrs J.F. Bishop (Isabella L. Bird), FRGS

Isabella's wupan

"I left the capital [Chengtu] *in a small flat-bottomed wupan, drawing four inches of water, with a mat roof, and without doors at either end. Yet my cambric curtains were never lifted, and when I desired it I enjoyed complete privacy at the expense of partial asphyxiation. At the time, May 20, the water was so low that no bigger boat could make the passage, and numbers of small, trim house-boats were aground."*

1896

Gelatin silver print

11.2 x 15.8cm

Text from *The Yangtze Valley and Beyond,* by Mrs J.F. Bishop (Isabella L. Bird), FRGS

West gate, Chia-ling Fu

*"Chia-ling Fu, said to be a city of 50,000 souls, is a place of great importance commercially, as
three large rivers – the Min, Ya, and Tatu – there form a junction, and for a brief space the river
is like a lake. It is perhaps the greatest centre of sericulture* and silk weaving in the province,
and is also the eastern boundary of the white wax trade. Its white silks are remarkable for
lustre and purity of colour. It is a rich city, and the capital of one of the most fertile and lovely
regions on earth."*

* The rearing of silkworms for the production of raw silk.

1896

Gelatin silver print

15.1 x 10.8cm

Text from *The Yangtze Valley and Beyond*, by Mrs J.F. Bishop (Isabella L. Bird), FRGS

A boat on the River Min, used for running the rapids

"The Min river, called also the Fu, is a western tributary of the Upper Yangtze, but a great river in itself. Of the boat's four sails the lowest is of bamboo, and is let down at night to protect the boatman and his family. The feature of the boat is its high prow, for protection against the rocks and rushing water."

This image was used in *The Yangtze Valley and Beyond*, but was taken by Dr Kinnear.

1896

Gelatin silver print

15 x 10.4cm

Text from *Chinese Pictures: Notes on Photographs Made in China*, by Mrs J.F. Bishop FRGS

Goddess of Mercy, wayside shrine, upper Min

*"Found all over the country, and commonly known as 'Joss Houses.' There is an idol in
each of them. They are of interest as presenting a similar feature to the shrine and wayside
crucifixes found all over Catholic countries in Europe."*

1896
Gelatin silver print
15 x 10.5cm
Text from *Chinese Pictures: Notes on Photographs Made in China*, by Mrs J.F. Bishop FRGS

ISABELLA BIRD

Stone Lion on tomb, Min river

"The lovely country was a very great charm. The variety of scenery, trees, flowers, and cultivated plants was endless, and new industries were constantly beoming prominent. The only matter for regret was that the rush of the fast-rising river carried us all too swiftly past much that was worthy of observation."

1896

Gelatin silver print

15.6 x 11cm

Text from *The Yangtze Valley and Beyond*, by Mrs J.F. Bishop (Isabella L. Bird), FRGS

Isabella's boat moored by a temple on a promontory, Min river

"Except for the heat, the downward journey was quite delightful; the country is so fertile and beautiful, and has such an air of prosperity. So long as we were in motion there was a draught, as the boat was quite open, but the still nights were stifling, specially with the curtains down. The boatmen were harmless, good-natured, obliging fellows. They tied up whenever I wanted to land if it were at all possible, and though they were obliged to pass from bow to stern through my 'room,' they always asked leave to do so if the curtains were down."

1896

Gelatin silver print

10.6 x 15cm

Text from *The Yangtze Valley and Beyond*, by Mrs J.F. Bishop (Isabella L. Bird), FRGS

"The American Baptists and the China Inland Mission do mission work in Sui Fu, and a great deal of valuable medical work. Though 'child-eating,' as elsewhere, is believed in, the people are not unfriendly, and the mandarin was specially courteous. Before I left he sent round to all the street officers to say that, whether I went through the city in a chair or on foot, there was to be no crowding, following, or staring. He sent four chai-jen in official hats to walk in front of me, and go down with me to Luchow, and two petty officers to see that no one interfered with my camera, on pain of being beaten."

Gate keeper of the China Inland Mission House, Sui Fu

1896
Gelatin silver print
15.2 x 10.7cm
Text from *The Yangtze Valley and Beyond*, by Mrs J.F. Bishop (Isabella L. Bird), FRGS

Pagoda near Luchow

"On the brilliant afternoon of the day after leaving Sui Fu, I reached Luchow, an important trading city, with a reputed population of 130,000. It is prettily situated on rising ground at the confluence of the Yangtze and To rivers."

1896

Gelatin silver print

15.4 x 9.9cm

Text from *The Yangtze Valley and Beyond*, by Mrs J.F. Bishop (Isabella L. Bird), FRGS

Fishing village, Upper Yangtze

"The force and volume of the river, which had then risen about forty-five feet above its winter level, were tremendous."

The horizontal banding on this image is on the original photograph, possibly the effect of a very slow exposure time on wave action.

1896

Gelatin silver print

10 x 15.4cm

Text from *The Yangtze Valley and Beyond*, by Mrs J.F. Bishop (Isabella L. Bird), FRGS

Wall of Chungking,
with gate towers

*"Whether Chungking (altitude 1,050ft.)
is approached from above or below, it
is a most striking city. It is surprising to
find, 1,500 miles inland, a town ot trom
400,000 to 500,000 people, including 2,500
Mohammedans, as the commercial capital
of Western China, one of the busiest cities
of the empire."*

1896

Gelatin silver print

10.8 x 15cm

Text from *The Yangtze Valley and Beyond*, by Mrs J.F. Bishop

(Isabella L. Bird), FRGS

"The military are usually dressed in picturesque but unserviceable, not to say grotesque costumes, the carnation red, beloved of the Chinese, and blue being the prevailing colours. They carry fans, and often paper umbrellas. They are ill-trained and indolent, lounging about the gates of the cities or the streets gambling and smoking. Their curse is that they have nothing to do."

Chungking soldiers, customs guard

1896

Gelatin silver print

15.1 x 10.8cm

Text from *Chinese Pictures: Notes on Photographs Made in China*, by Mrs J.F. Bishop FRGS

'Stone Precious Castle', Shi-pao-chai

"I landed also at Shi-pao-chai ('Stone Precious Castle'), a place of pilgrimage. The south-east side of the rock (not given in the illustration) has a nine-storeyed pavilion, resting on a very strikingly decorated temple built against it, through which access to the summit is gained. On the flat top there is a temple of three courts. The pavilion building has curved and decorated roofs, and looks like a magnificent eleven-storeyed pagoda. A large village lies at its feet. My films were spotted with damp, and would have failed anyhow, owing to the overpowering curiosity of the people. The rock and its talus are about 300 feet in height."

1896

Gelatin silver print

10.9 x 15.2cm

Text from *The Yangtze Valley and Beyond*, by Mrs J.F. Bishop (Isabella L. Bird), FRGS

Pagoda on the Yangtze

"When we reached rapids, five men pulled frantically with yells which posed as songs, to keep steerage way on her, and we went down like a flash – down smooth hills of water, where rapids had been obliterated; down leaping races, where they had been created; past hideous whirlpools, where to have been sucked in would have been destruction; past temples, pagodas, and grey cities on heights; past villages gleaming white midst dense greenery; past hill, valley, woodland, garden cultivation, and signs of industry and prosperity; past frantic crews, straining at the sweeps, chanting wildly, bound downwards like ourselves; and still for days the Great River hurried us on remorselessly along. There was no time to take in anything. A pagoda or city scarcely appeared before it vanished…"

1896

Gelatin silver print

14.3 x 10cm

Text from *The Yangtze Valley and Beyond*, by Mrs J.F. Bishop (Isabella L. Bird), FRGS

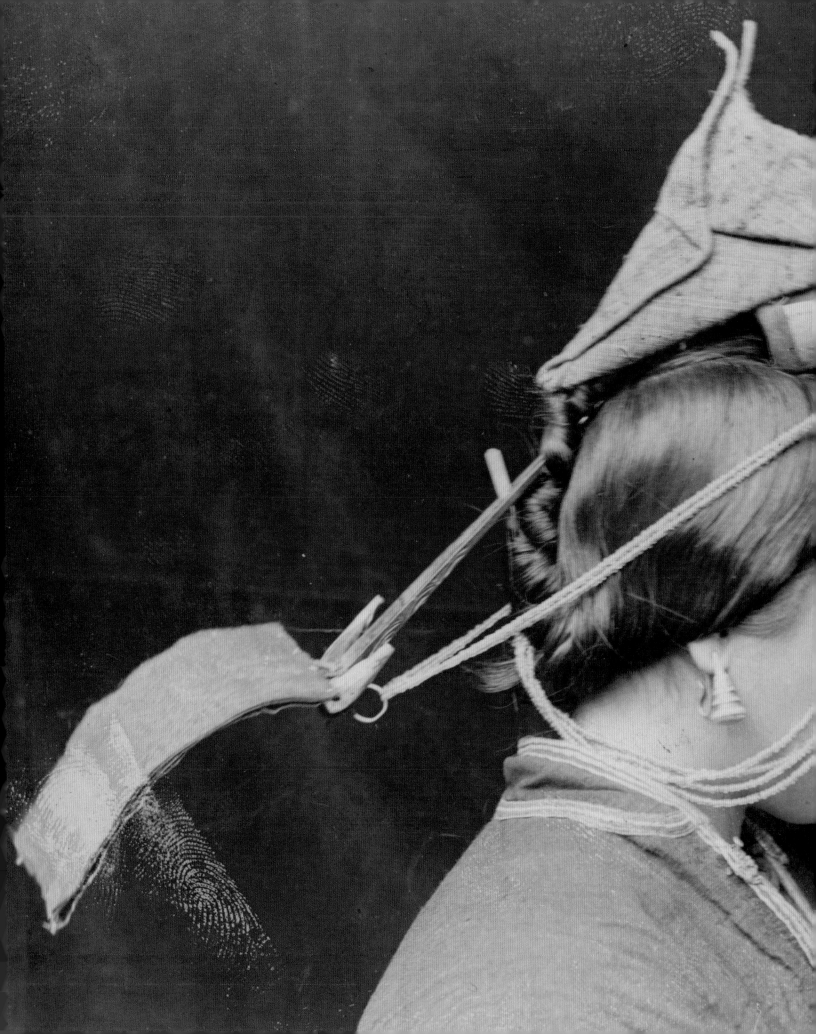

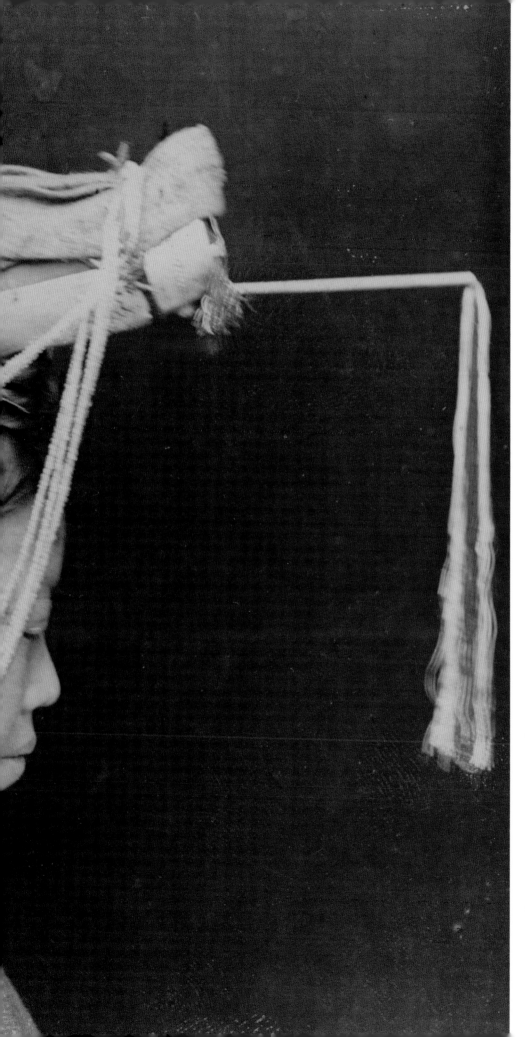

Gala headdress, 'dog-faced' woman

"This term 'dog-faced,' apparently does not bear the meaning which we put on it, for the woman in the illustration with a head-dress of solid silver and heavy white silk from the mountains of Fu Kien is a member of what the Fu-chow Chinese call 'dog-faced' tribes."

This image was used in *The Yangtze Valley and Beyond,* but was taken by Dr Kinnear.

1896

Gelatin silver print

9.8 x 14.3cm

Text from *The Yangtze Valley and Beyond*, by Mrs J.F. Bishop (Isabella L. Bird), FRGS

Lantern Slides

Woman reeling silk

Circa 1894–96

Reproduced in *The Yangtze Valley and Beyond*, by Mrs J.F. Bishop (Isabella L. Bird), FRGS

A lantern slide is a positive transparency made from an original negative and intended for projection in a magic lantern. The glass slide is coated with a light-sensitive material, exposed to the negative, developed and fixed. A second piece of clear glass provides a protective cover and is taped in place. This gives the slide a characteristic look and weighty feel when handled.

Lantern slides became popular in the mid-nineteenth century. For her talk on 'A Journey in Western Sze-chuan' to the Royal Geographical Society on 10th May, 1897, Isabella used 40 lantern slides prepared by the Royal Geographical Society from her own negatives. The numbered black and white slides reproduced here are some of those used in the talk.

Before the advent of film and television, lantern slides provided audiences with their first views of people and places from around the world. They were an important medium for photographers, and by 1900 Isabella had taken lessons in making her own slides. While not accurate, hand colouring of slides could create more drama and impact, and an added element of entertainment for viewers.

Manzu house. 65 28

Headman's house, Chu-ti

1896

Reproduced in *The Yangtze Valley and Beyond*, by Mrs J.F. Bishop (Isabella L. Bird), FRGS

Dragon Bridge. Sintien. 65 19

A Dragon bridge

1896

Reproduced in *The Yangtze Valley and Beyond* and *Chinese Pictures*

Manzu Country. 65 41

Square Tower, Somo

1896

Reproduced in *The Yangtze Valley and Beyond*, by Mrs J.F. Bishop (Isabella L. Bird), FRGS

Bridge at Awan Hsien. 65.37
S0015161

Bridge at Wan Hsien

1896

Reproduced in *The Yangtze Valley and Beyond*, by Mrs J. F. Bishop (Isabella L. Bird), FRGS

Coloured lantern slides from the Sir Walter C. Hillier
Collection at The Royal Geographical Society (with IBG).[1]

Coffins awaiting burial

1896

Reproduced in *The Yangtze Valley and Beyond* and *Chinese Pictures*

Xuanwu gate, Peking

1894

A mule cart

1894

Reproduced in *Chinese Pictures: Notes on Photographs Made in China*, by Mrs J.F. Bishop FRGS

God of Thunder, Lin-Yang

1895

Similar image reproduced in *The Yangtze Valley and Beyond*,

by Mrs J.F. Bishop (Isabella L. Bird), FRGS

Junks at Foochow

1895

The Temple of the God of Literature at Mukden

1894

Reproduced in *Chinese Pictures: Notes on Photographs Made in China*,

by Mrs J.F. Bishop FRGS

The entrance to the British Legation, Peking

1894

Reproduced in *Chinese Pictures: Notes on Photographs Made in China*,

by Mrs J.F. Bishop FRGS

A foot boat found in Central China

Circa 1894–96

Reproduced in *Chinese Pictures: Notes on Photographs Made in China*,

by Mrs J. F. Bishop FRGS

Photographic Terms

CHINESE SOLDIERS.

The image depicting soldiers of the Viceroy's Guard, is shown as a lantern slide (above) used for lectures, the original photograph from which it was taken (right) and as an engraving (far right), which was reproduced as a book illustration in 1898.

Some of the terms used by Isabella many require some explanation. Processes that she enjoyed, such as enamelling, have completely disappeared but are worth explaining.

Enamelling

Enamelling was a type of finishing process that gave a brilliance to a print. A description of enamelling is given in *The Art and Practice of Silver Printing* by H. P. Robinson and Captain Abney, a copy of which can be found in the National Library of Scotland. The description below is taken from that book:

"There are several modes of enamelling prints, but there is none better than that described by Mr. W. England, which we quote in his words. "I have a glass having a good polished surface (patent plate is not necessary), and rub over it some powdered French chalk tied up in a muslin bag. Dust off the superfluous chalk with a camel's hair brush, and coat with enamel collodion. I find it an improvement to add to the collodion usually sold for the purpose 2 dr. of castor oil to the pint. When the collodion is well set, immerse the plate in a dish of water. When several prints are required to be enamelled, a sufficient number of plates may be prepared and put in dishes; this will save time. Now take the first plate, and well wash under a tap till all greasiness has disappeared; place it on a levelling stand, and pour on as much water as the plate will hold. Then lay the print on the top, squeeze out all the water, and place the plate and print between several thicknesses of blotting-paper to remove all superfluous moisture. The plate, with the print in contact, should now be placed in a warm room to dry spontaneously, when the print will come easily from the glass. Care should be taken not to attempt to remove the print*

till quite dry. If the pictures required to be enamelled have been dried, it will be necessary to rub over them some ox-gall with a plug of soft rag; otherwise the water will run in globules on the surface, and make blisters when laid on the collodion."

Gelatin Silver Print

A gelatin silver print is made on paper coated with gelatin, which holds light-sensitive silver salts. The salts react when exposed to light, producing an image when contact printed with a negative.

Negatives

Once exposed in the camera, negatives, either glass or celluloid, were developed with chemical compounds and fixed before photographic prints could be made. Isabella describes using the fast flowing waters of the Yangtze to wash the hypo, the fixing agent, from the negative, using filtered water for a final rinse to remove any silt, which might have settled on the negative.

Printing Frames

Printing frames were used to expose a negative to paper coated with light-sensitive silver salts. Isabella describes hanging the printing frames over the side of the boat. Photographs created in this way are contact printed, the resulting photographic print being the exact same size as the negative.

Printing-out Paper

For convenience, Isabella may have used printing-out paper when travelling on the Yangtze. Printing-out paper requires no chemical to aid the development, just a light source, washing and toning.

Toning

Toning is a process that can take place either when a photograph is being developed or after development. It is a process that affects the colour of the print. Metals in the toning solution replace those originally exposed and it can greatly enhance the appearance of a print, increasing contrast and changing colour depending on the metals used. Isabella appears to have toned her photographs after development.

Retouching images

When working with archive photographs in publications it is tempting to clean up images, removing any imperfections with Photoshop.

There is a dilemma in this approach as the resulting image can look super-clean, and the clues to the history and the integrity of the original disappear with the dust and scratches. So the images in this book have not been retouched.

Chronology

1831

15th October: Isabella Lucy Bird born at Boroughbridge Hall, North Yorkshire to Edward Bird and Dora Bird (*née* Lawson).

1833

Birth of brother, Edward Bird, who dies in the same year.

1834

Birth of sister, Henrietta Amelia Bird, in Tattenhall, Cheshire.

1848

Family moves to Wyton, Huntingdon.

1849

Isabella writes a pamphlet on Free Trade and publishes it herself, at the age of 18.

1850

Isabella undergoes an operation on her spine to remove a fibrous tumour.

1854

First major journey to America, undertaken by Isabella at the age of 23.

1855

An introduction to publisher John Murray III results in Isabella's first book commission.

1850–64

Taiping Rebellion, a civil war in China, which results in the death of approximately 20 million civilians and soldiers.

1856

The Englishwoman in America, based on Isabella's first major foreign journey, is published by John Murray.

1857

Second journey to North America.

1858

14th May: Edward Bird dies suddenly of influenza in Wyton, Huntingdon.

1859

The Aspects of Religion in the United States, published by Samson, Low, Son and Co.

1860

Dora Bird rents a flat at 3 Castle Terrace, Edinburgh.

1861–65

American Civil War.

1866

Dora Bird dies in Edinburgh.

1869

Notes on Old Edinburgh

published by Edmonston & Douglas, Edinburgh.

1872

Isabella visits Maine and New York, in the United States, returning via the Mediterranean ports in Italy, Algeria, Spain and Portugal.

Isabella and her sister give up the flat at Castle Terrace, Edinburgh.

11th June: Isabella leaves Edinburgh for Australia.

1873

Isabella returns via New Zealand, Hawaii (where she spends seven months) and Colorado (four months).

Publication of first two volumes of *Illustrations of China and its People* by John Thomson.

1874

The sisters rent a flat, where Isabella writes a book based on her experiences in Hawaii.

1875

The Hawaiian Archipelago: Six Months Among the Palm Groves, Coral Reefs and Volcanoes of the Sandwich Islands is published by John Murray.

February: a favourable review of *The Hawaiian Archipelago* is published in the journal *Nature*.

1877

To honour the memory of David Livingstone (1813–73), the National Livingstone Memorial is founded to train medical missionaries; both Isabella and Henrietta become involved in fund raising.

1878

Isabella makes her first visit to Japan, travelling via New York and Shanghai.

1879

On her way home via Hong Kong and Canton, Isabella travels by steamer to the Malay States, returning via Cairo and Sinai, where she contracts typhoid fever. Seriously ill, she is nursed on her return by Henrietta.

A Lady's Life in the Rocky Mountains is published by John Murray.

1880

Unbeaten Tracks in Japan is published by John Murray.

5th June: Henrietta dies of typhoid fever.

1881

8th March: Isabella marries Dr John Bishop while still in deep mourning for her sister.

1883

The Golden Chersonese and the Way Thither is published by John Murray.

1884

Convention between Japan and China reduces Korea to a virtual co-protectorate.

1886

6th March: John Bishop dies.

John Thomson is appointed Instructor of Photography at the Royal Geographical Society.

1889

Isabella travels to Islamabad to set up a hospital dedicated to John Bishop and a dispensary commemorating Henrietta. Her journey on to Western Tibet forms the basis of *Among the Tibetans*.

1890

Isabella returns via Persia (where she joins a military-geographical mission), Kurdistan and Turkey.

The Royal Geographical Society purchases a magic lantern for illustrating talks and lectures.

1891

21st April: Isabella dines with Prime Minister William Gladstone.

Travels in Persia and Kurdistan is published by John Murray.

Isabella is awarded Fellowship of the Royal Scottish Geographical Society.

Isabella gives a Christmas lecture to the people of Tobermory.

1892

Journeys in Persia and Kurdistan (two volumes) is published by John Murray.

2nd April, John Murray III dies.

June: Isabella takes instruction in photography from Howard Farmer, head of photography at Regent Street Polytechnic.

28th November: Isabella is elected Fellow of the Royal Geographical Society.

1893

Isabella learns how to make prints from her own negatives. Isabella is presented to Queen Victoria.

1894

Among the Tibetans is published by John Murray.

11th January: Isabella travels to Yokohama, Japan and on to Korea, using Seoul as a base for her exploration of the country.

21st June: Isabella is deported following Japanese occupation

of Korea, travelling to China and visiting Chefoo, Newchwang and Mukden.

1st August: China and Japan declare war.

20th August: Isabella leaves Mukden for Peking.

October: All European women are ordered to leave Peking. Isabella travels to Vladivostock.

December: Isabella visits Japan.

1895

January: Isabella spends time in Seoul, Korea.

February: Isabella travels to Hong Kong to begin a tour of church missions.

17th April: Peace treaty signed by China and Japan.

June: Isabella travels to Japan.

October: Isabella travels to Korea.

1896

January: Isabella travels to Shanghai, China to begin her journey on the Yangtze.

May: Isabella leaves Chengtu Fu to return to Shanghai.

June: Isabella arrives in Shanghai.

July: Isabella travels to Japan.

1897

Isabella becomes a member of the Royal Photographic Society.

Views in the Far East is published by S. Kajima, Tokyo, Japan.

Isabella returns from China.

10th May: Isabella gives a Royal Geographical Society lecture, titled 'A Journey in Western Sze-Chuan'.

1898

Korea and Her Neighbours (two volumes) is published by John Murray.

1899

The Yangtze Valley and Beyond is published by John Murray.

1900

Chinese Pictures is published by Cassell and Co.

1901

Isabella travels to Morocco.

1902

Isabella takes advanced photographic lessons in enlarging photographs.

1903

Isabella returns to Edinburgh; her health deteriorates drastically.

1904

7th October: Isabella dies in Edinburgh, aged 72.

Bibliography

Abney, William de Wiveleslie, Sir, and Robinson, Henry Peach, *The Art and Practice of Silver Printing*, London, Piper and Carter, 1881.

Badger, Gerry, and Parr, Martin, *The Photobook: A History, Volume 1*, London, Phaidon Press, 2004.

Baldwin, Gordon, *Looking at Photographs, a Guide to Technical Terms*, The J. Paul Getty Museum in association with British Museum Press, 1991.

Barr, Pat, *A Curious Life for a Lady, The Story of Isabella Bird*, London, John Murray, 1970.

Bird, Isabella L., *The Englishwoman in America*, London, John Murray, 1856.

Bird, Isabella L., *The Aspects of Religion in the United States*, Samson, Low, Son and Co., 1859.

Bird, Isabella, L., *Notes on Old Edinburgh*, Edinburgh, Edmonston & Douglas, 1869.

Bird, Isabella, L., *The Hawaiian Archipelago, Six Months Among the Palm Groves, Coral Reefs, and Volcanoes of the Sandwich Islands*, London, John Murray, 1875.

Bird, Isabella, L., *A Lady's Life in the Rocky Mountains*, London, John Murray, 1879.

Bird, Isabella, L., *Unbeaten Tracks in Japan*, London, John Murray, 1880.

Bird, Isabella, L. (Mrs Bishop), *The Golden Chersonese and the Way Thither*, London, John Murray, 1883.

Bishop, Mrs (Isabella, L. Bird), *Travels in Persia and Kurdistan*, London, John Murray, 1891.

Bishop, Mrs (Isabella, L. Bird), *Journeys in Persia and Kurdistan*, Volumes 1 and 2, London, John Murray, 1892.

Bishop, Mrs (Isabella L. Bird), FRGS, *Among the Tibetans*, London, The Religious Tract Society, 1894.

Bishop, Mrs (Isabella, L. Bird), *Views in the Far East*, Japan, S. Kajima, Tokyo, 1897.

Bishop, Mrs (Isabella L. Bird), FRGS, *Korea and Her Neighbours,* Volumes 1 and 2, London, John Murray, 1898.

Bishop, Mrs J.F. (Isabella L. Bird FRPS), *The Yangtze Valley and Beyond*, London, John Murray, 1899.

Bishop, Mrs J.F., FRGS, *Chinese Pictures*, London, Cassell and Co., 1900.

Cameron, Ian, *To the Farthest Ends of the Earth*, New York, Dutton, 1980.

Carpenter, Humphrey, *Seven Lives of John Murray: The Story of a Publishing Dynasty 1768–2002*, London, John Murray, 2009.

Checkland, Olive, *Isabella Bird (1831–1904) 'and a woman's right to do what she can do well'*, Aberdeen, Scottish Cultural Press, 1996.

Christie, Dugald, *Thirty years in Moukden 1883–1913, Being the Experiences and Recollections of Dugald Christie C.M.G.*, London, Constable and Co., 1914.

Chubbuck, Kay, ed., *Isabella Bird: Letters to Henrietta*, London, John Murray, 2002.

Cooper, James Fenimore, *The Last of the Mohicans*, Philadelphia, Carey and Lea, 1826.

Eliot, George, *Middlemarch*, Edinburgh and London, William Blackwood and Sons, 1871–72.

Farr, William, *Vital Statistics*, London, The Sanitary Institute of Great Britain and Edward Stanford, 1885.

Freshfield, D.W., and Wharton, W.J.L., *Hints to Travellers, Scientific and General*, 6th edition, London, Royal Geographical Society, 1889.

Hall, Captain Basil, *Travels in North America 1827–1828*, Edinburgh, Cadell and Co., and London, Simpkin and Marshall, 1829.

Hannavy, John, *Encyclopedia of Nineteenth-Century Photography*, Volume 1, Routledge Taylor & Francis Group, 2008.

Hsu, Immanuel C.Y., *The Rise of Modern China*, Oxford, Oxford University Press, 1990.

Middleton, Dorothy, *Victorian Lady Travellers*, London, Routledge & Kegan Paul, 1965.

Stoddart, Anna M., *The Life of Isabella Bird (Mrs Bishop)*, London, John Murray, 1906.

Teeple, John B., *Timelines of World History*, Dorling Kindersley, 2002.

Thomson, John, *The Antiquities of Cambodia*, Edinburgh, Edmonston & Douglas, 1867.

Thomson, John, *Illustrations of China and its People*, London, Sampson Low, Marston, Low, and Searle, 1874 and 1875.

Thomson, John, *The Straits of Malacca, Indo-China and China, or Ten Years' Travels, Adventures and Residence Abroad*, London, Sampson Low, Marston, Low, and Searle, 1875.

Thomson, John, *Through China With a Camera*, London, Constable, 1898.

Trollope, Frances, *Domestic Manners of America*, London, Whittaker, Teacher, & Co., 1832.

Wheeler, Sara, *O My America! Second Acts in a New World*, London, Jonathan Cape, 2013.

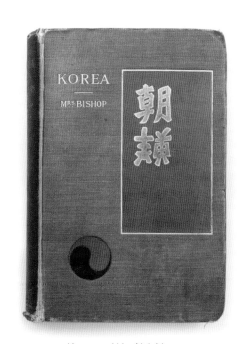

Korea and Her Neighbours

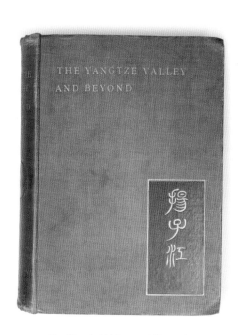

The Yangtze Valley and Beyond

Notes

A Traveller's Tales

Pages 10 to 15

[1] West, Richard, *Spectator* book review, 'Cattleman and Devil man', 9th July, 1982, http://archive.spectator.co.uk/article/10th-july-1982/22/cattleman-and-devil-man.

[2] Isabella L. Bird to Henrietta Bird, 19th February, 1873, Ms. 42020, John Murray Archive, National Library of Scotland.

[3] Isabella L. Bird to John Murray III, 13th December, 1873, Ms. 42024, John Murray Archive, National Library of Scotland.

[4] Stoddart, Anna M., *The Life of Isabella Bird (Mrs Bishop)*, London, John Murray, 1906, 21.

[5] *Spectator*, 'Rocky Mountain Romance', a review of the first edition of *A Lady's Life in the Rocky Mountains*, 8th November, 1879.

[6] Checkland, Olive, *Isabella Bird (1831–1904) 'and a Woman's Right To Do What She Can Do Well'*, Aberdeen, Scottish Cultural Press, 1996, 29.

[7] Farr, William, *Vital Statistics*, 'Annual Marriage-rate of Batchelors, Spinsters, Widowers & Widows at different ages in 1851 and the three years 1870–72', London, The Sanitary Institute of Great Britain and Edward Stanford, 1885, 80.

[8] *The Times*, book review of *A Lady's Life in the Rocky Mountains*, 22nd November, 1879

[9] Barr, Pat, *A Curious Life for a Lady, The Story of Isabella Bird*, London, John Murray, 1970, 185.

[10] Stoddart, Anna M., *The Life of Isabella Bird (Mrs Bishop)*, London, John Murray, 1906, 51.

[11] *The Times*, letter to the editor headed 'Distress in Edinburgh', appealing for subscriptions for a small public laundry, 8th June, 1871.

[12] Stoddart, Anna M., *The Life of Isabella Bird (Mrs Bishop)*, London, John Murray, 1906, 49.

[13] Bird, Isabella L., *Notes on Old Edinburgh*, Edinburgh, Edmonston & Douglas, 1869.

[14] Isabella L. Bird to Henrietta Bird, 13th October, 1872, Ms. 42020, John Murray Archive, National Library of Scotland.

[15] Isabella L. Bird to Henrietta Bird, 27th October, 1872, Ms. 42020, John Murray Archive, National Library of Scotland.

16. Cooper, James Fenimore, *The Last of the Mohicans*, Philadelphia, Carey and Lea, 1826.

[17] Chubbuck, Kay, *Letters to Henrietta*, London, John Murray, 2002, 331.

[18] Isabella L. Bird to Henrietta Bird, 4th December, 1873, Ms. 42020, John Murray Archive, National Library of Scotland.

[19] Eliot, George, *Middlemarch*, Edinburgh and London, Willliam Blackwood and Sons, 1871–72. The novel appeared in serial form between 1871 and 1872, and was published as a single-volume edition in 1874. See Doreen Roberts' introduction and notes, *Middlemarch Wordsworth Classic*, 2000.

[20] Hall, Captain Basil, *Travels in North America 1827–1828*, Edinburgh, Cadell and Co., and London, Simpkin and Marshall, 1829.

[21] Trollope, Frances, *Domestic Manners of America*, London, Whittaker, Teacher, & Co., 1832.

[22] Stoddart, Anna M., *The Life of Isabella Bird (Mrs Bishop)*, London, John Murray, 1906, 15.

[23] Bird, Isabella L., *The Hawaiian Archipelago: Six Months Among the Palm Groves, Coral Reefs, and Volcanoes of the Sandwich Islands*, London, John Murray, 1875, 10.

[24] Chubbuck, Kay, *Letters to Henrietta*, London, John Murray, 2002, 13.

[25] Isabella L. Bird, circular letter sent from Persia, 24th December, 1889, Ms. 42023 John Murray Archive, National Library of Scotland.

[26] Isabella L. Bird to Henrietta Bird, 13th July, 1873, Ms. 42020, John Murray Archive, National Library of Scotland.

[27] Isabella L. Bird to Henrietta Bird, 29th October, 1873, Ms. 42020, John Murray Archive, National Library of Scotland.

[28] Curzon, George, *The Times*, 'Ladies and The Royal Geographical Society', 31st May, 1893, London.

[29] Isabella L. Bird to John Scott Keltie, 4th December, 1897, CB7/22, Royal Geographical Society Library.

A Passion for Photography

Pages 16 to 23

[1] Isabella L. Bishop to John Murray IV, 7th February, 1894 (not sent until 2nd December), Ms. 42028 f 29, John Murray Archive, National Library of Scotland.

[2] Isabella L. Bishop to John Murray IV, 23rd January, 1897, Ms. 42028 f 29, John Murray Archive, National Library of Scotland.

[3] Bishop, Mrs J.F. (Isabella L. Bird FRPS), *The Yangtze Valley and Beyond*, London, John Murray, London, 1899, 122.

[4] Stoddart, Anna M., *The Life of Isabella Bird (Mrs Bishop)*, London, John Murray, 1906, 298.

[5] Freshfield, Douglas, and Mill, Dr Hugh Robert, *The Geographical Journal*, Vol. 69, No. 3, 281–287, obituary of Sir John Scott Keltie. Keltie served as assistant secretary of the Royal Geographical Society from 1892 to 1896, then as secretary, 1896–1915.

[6] *Nature*, No. 119, 22nd January, 1927, 130–133, obituary of Sir John Scott Keltie.

[7] Cameron, Ian, *To the Farthest Ends of the Earth*, New York, Dutton, 1980, 204.

[8] Certificate of Candidate for Election (elected 28th November, 1892), Royal Geographical Society Library.

[9] Isabella L. Bishop to John Scott Keltie, 10th March, 1897, CB7/6, Royal Geographical Society Library.

[10] Badger, Gerry, and Parr, Martin, *The Photobook: A History*, Volume 1, London, Phaidon Press, 2004, 32.

[11] Parker, Elliot S., *The Geographical Journal*, Vol. 144, No. 3, 469, 'John Thomson 1837–1921 Royal Geographical Scoiety Instructor in Photography'.

[12] Freshfield, D.W., and Wharton, W.J.L., *Hints to Travellers, Scientific and General*, 6th edition, London, Royal Geographical Society, 1889.

[13] Stoddart, Anna M., *The Life of Isabella Bird (Mrs Bishop)*, London, John Murray, 1906, 259.

[14] Stoddart, Anna M., *The Life of Isabella Bird (Mrs Bishop)*, London, John Murray, 1906, 266.

15 Isabella L. Bishop to John Murray IV, 23rd January, 1897, Ms. 42028 f 29, John Murray Archive, National Library of Scotland.

16 Bishop, Mrs J.F. (Isabella L. Bird FRPS), *The Yangtze Valley and Beyond*, London, John Murray, 1899, 422.

17 Freshfield, D.W., and Wharton, W.J.L., *Hints to Travellers, Scientific and General*, 6th edition, London, Royal Geographical Society, 1889.

18 Bishop, Mrs J.F. (Isabella L. Bird FRPS), *The Yangtze Valley and Beyond*, London, John Murray, 1899, 117.

19 Freshfield, D.W., and Wharton, W.J.L., *Hints to Travellers, Scientific and General*, 6th edition, London, Royal Geographical Society, 1889.

20 Mrs Bishop (Isabella L. Bird), *Korea and Her Neighbours*, Volume 1, London, John Murray, 1898, 71.

21 Bishop, Mrs J.F. (Isabella L. Bird FRPS), *The Yangtze Valley and Beyond*, London, John Murray, 1899, 83.

22 Bishop, Mrs J.F. (Isabella L. Bird FRPS), *The Yangtze Valley and Beyond*, London, John Murray, 1899, 156.

23 Stoddart, Anna M., *The Life of Isabella Bird (Mrs Bishop)*, London, John Murray, 1906, 298.

24 Stoddart, Anna M., *The Life of Isabella Bird (Mrs Bishop)*, London, John Murray, 1906, 299.

25 Isabella L. Bishop to John Scott Keltie, 5th October, 1894, CB7/5, Royal Geographical Society Library.

26 Bishop, Mrs J.F. (Isabella L. Bird FRPS), *The Yangtze Valley and Beyond*, London, John Murray, 1899, 117.

27 Bishop, Mrs J.F. (Isabella L. Bird FRPS), *The Yangtze Valley and Beyond*, London, John Murray, 1899, 195.

28 Bishop, Mrs J.F. (Isabella L. Bird FRPS), *The Yangtze Valley and Beyond*, London, John Murray, 1899, 252.

29 Isabella L. Bishop to John Scott Keltie, 4th December, 1897, CB7/22, Royal Geographical Society Library.

30 Royal Scottish Geographical Society, *The Times*, London, 14th November, 1891.

31 Hannavy, John, *Encyclopedia of Nineteenth-Century Photography*, Volume 1, 'Royal Geographical Society, The World Through a Lens', Routledge Taylor & Francis Group, 2008, 1217.

32 Mill, Dr Hugh Robert, *The Record of the Royal Geographical Society, 1830–1930*, October, 1930, London, Royal Geographical Society.

33 Isabella L. Bishop to John Scott Keltie, 29th April, 1897, CB7/14, Royal Geographical Society Library: 'I left about 40 negatives for Lantern Slides with Mr Simpson', in preparation for her paper read at the Royal Geographical Society, 10th May, 1897.

34 Isabella L. Bishop to John Scott Keltie, 4th December, 1897, CB7/20, Royal Geographical Society Library.

35 Isabella L. Bishop to Mrs Blackie, 27th December, 1891, Ms. 2638 f 294–298, John Murray Archive, National Library of Scotland.

36 Isabella L. Bishop to John Murray IV, 7th February, 1894 (not sent until 2nd December), Ms. 42028 f 29, John Murray Archive, National Library of Scotland.

37 Thomson, John, *The Antiquities of Cambodia, A series of photographs taken on the spot with letterpress description*, Edinburgh, Edmonston & Douglas, 1867.

38 Thomson, John, *Illustrations of China and its People: A series of two hundred photographs, with letterpress descriptive of the places and people represented*, four volumes, London, Sampson Low, Marston, Low, and Searle, London, 1874 and 1875.

39 Thomson, John, *The Straits of Malacca, Indo-China and China or Ten Years' Travels, Adventures and Residence Abroad*, London, Sampson Low, Marston, Low, and Searle, 1875.

40 Isabella L. Bishop to John Murray IV, 11th April, 1896, Ms. 42028 f 21, John Murray Archive, National Library of Scotland.

41 Isabella L. Bishop to John Murray IV, 6th July, 1896, Ms. 42028 f 22, John Murray Archive, National Library of Scotland.

42 Isabella L. Bishop to John Murray IV, 6th July, 1896, Ms. 42028 f 22, John Murray Archive, National Library of Scotland.

43 Isabella L. Bishop to John Murray III, 29th October, 1891, Ms. 42027 f 76, John Murray Archive, National Library of Scotland.

44 Stoddart, Anna M., *The Life of Isabella Bird (Mrs Bishop)*, London, John Murray, 1906, 327.

45 Bishop, Isabella L., *Views in the Far East*, Tokyo, Japan, S. Kajima, 1897.

46 Isabella L. Bishop to John Murray IV, 8th July, 1897, Ms. 42028 f 42, John Murray Archive, National Library of Scotland.

47 Contact printed from original half-plate negatives.

48 *Nature*, 14th January, 1875, 207–208, book review of John Thomson's *The Straits of Malacca, Indo-China and China or Ten Years' Travels, Adventures and Residence Abroad*; and *Nature*, February, 1875, 322–324, book review of Isabella L. Bird's *The Hawaiian Archipelago: Six Months Among the Palm Groves, Coral Reefs and Volcanoes of the Sandwich Islands*.

49 Bishop, Mrs J.F. (Isabella L. Bird FRPS), *The Yangtze Valley and Beyond*, London, John Murray, 1899, 166.

50 Bishop, Mrs J.F. (Isabella L. Bird FRPS), *The Yangtze Valley and Beyond*, London, John Murray, 1899, 210.

51 Isabella L. Bishop to John Murray IV, 7th February, 1894 (not sent until 2nd December), Ms. 42028 f 29, John Murray Archive, National Library of Scotland.

52 Isabella L. Bishop was elected to membership of the Royal Photographic Society on 12th January, 1897, taken from information on the RPS membership 1843–1900 database, compiled by Dr Michael Pritchard.

53 Isabella L. Bishop to John Scott Keltie, 10th March, 1897, CB7/6, Royal Geographical Society Library.

A Chinese Odyssey

Pages 24 to 35

[1] Bishop, Mrs J.F. (Isabella L. Bird FRPS), *The Yangtze Valley and Beyond*, London, John Murray, 1899, 11.

[2] Teeple, John B., *Timelines of World History*, Dorling Kindersley, 2002, 380.

[3] Hsu, Immanuel C.Y., *The Rise of Modern China*, Oxford, Oxford University Press, 1990, 337.

[4] Stoddart, Anna M., *The Life of Isabella Bird (Mrs Bishop)*, London, John Murray, 1906, 275.

[5] Isabella L. Bishop to John Murray IV, 23rd August, 1893, Ms. 42027 f 112, John Murray Archive, National Library of Scotland.

[6] Isabella L. Bishop to John Scott Keltie, 5th October, 1894, CB7/5, Royal Geographical Society Library.

[7] Teeple, John B., *Timelines of Worlds History*, Dorling Kindersley, 2002, 380.

[8] Isabella L. Bishop to John Scott Keltie, 5th October, 1894, CB7/5, Royal Geographical Society Library.

[9] Mrs Bishop (Isabella L. Bird), *Korea and Her Neighbours*, Volume 1, London, John Murray, 1898, 207.

[10] Isabella L. Bishop to John Scott Keltie, 5th October, 1894, CB7/5, Royal Geographical Society Library.

[11] Christie, Dugald, *Thirty Years in Moukden 1883–1913, Being the Experiences and Recollections of Dugald Christie C.M.G.*, London, Constable and Co., 1914, 48.

[12] Christie, Dugald, *Thirty Years in Moukden 1883–1913, Being the Experiences and Recollections of Dugald Christie C.M.G.*, London, Constable and Co., 1914, 72.

[13] Mrs Bishop (Isabella L. Bird), *Korea and Her Neighbours*, Volume 1, London, John Murray, 1898, 238.

[14] Christie, Dugald, *Thirty Years in Moukden 1883–1913, Being the Experiences and Recollections of Dugald Christie C.M.G.*, London, Constable and Co., 1914, 24.

[15] *The Western Gazette*, 'An English Lady Among the Coreans', 3rd August, 1894, www.britishnewspaperarchive.co.uk.

[16] Hsu, Immanuel C. Y., *The Rise of Modern China*, Oxford, Oxford University Press, 1990, 340.

[17] Isabella L. Bishop to John Scott Keltie, 5th October, 1894, CB7/5, Royal Geographical Society Library.

[18] Stoddart, Anna M., *The Life of Isabella Bird (Mrs Bishop)*, London, John Murray, 1906, 289.

[19] *The North China Herald and Supreme Court & Consular Gazette*, 'A Lecture by Mrs Bishop', 5th October, 1894, 205.

[20] Isabella L. Bishop to John Scott Keltie, 5th October, 1894, CB7/5, Royal Geographical Society Library.

[21] Isabella L. Bishop, *The Times*, 'Foreigners in Pekin', London, 28th November, 1894.

[22] Isabella L. Bishop to John Scott Keltie, 5th October, 1894, CB7/5, Royal Geographical Society Library.

[23] Bishop, Mrs J.F. (Isabella L. Bird FRPS), *The Yangtze Valley and Beyond*, London, John Murray, 1899, 523.

[24] Bishop, Mrs J.F. (Isabella L. Bird FRPS), *The Yangtze Valley and Beyond*, London, John Murray, 1899, 527.

[25] Stoddart, Anna M., *The Life of Isabella Bird (Mrs Bishop)*, London, John Murray, 1906, 296.

[26] Isabella L. Bishop to John Murray IV, 27th May, 1895, Ms. 42028 f 10 VII 95, John Murray Archive, National Library of Scotland.

[27] Isabella L. Bishop to Mrs Blackie, 27th December, 1891, Ms. 2638 f 294–298, John Murray Archive, National Library of Scotland.

[28] Stoddart, Anna M., *The Life of Isabella Bird (Mrs Bishop)*, London, John Murray, 1906, 25.

[29] Isabella L. Bishop to John Murray IV, 22nd January, 1896, Ms. 42028 f John Murray Archive, National Library of Scotland.

[30] Carpenter, Humphrey, *The Seven Lives of John Murray: The Story of a Publishing Dynasty*, London, John Murray, 2009, 206.

[31] Bishop, Mrs J.F. (Isabella L. Bird FRPS), *The Yangtze Valley and Beyond*, London, John Murray, 1899, 5.

[32] Bishop, Mrs J.F. (Isabella L. Bird FRPS), *The Yangtze Valley and Beyond*, London, John Murray, 1899, 206.

[33] Bishop, Mrs J.F. (Isabella L. Bird FRPS), *The Yangtze Valley and Beyond*, London, John Murray, 1899, 220.

[34] Hsu, Immanuel C. Y., *The Rise of Modern China*, Oxford, Oxford University Press, 1990, 221.

[35] Isabella L. Bishop to John Murray IV, 6th June, 1896, Ms. 42028 f 22, John Murray Archive, National Library of Scotland.

[36] Bishop, Mrs J.F. (Isabella L. Bird FRPS), *The Yangtze Valley and Beyond*, London, John Murray, 1899, 501.

[37] Hsu, Immanuel C.Y., *The Rise of Modern China*, Oxford, Oxford University Press, 1990, 346.

[38] Bishop, Mrs J.F. (Isabella L. Bird FRPS), *The Yangtze Valley and Beyond*, London, John Murray, 1899, 530.

[39] Carpenter, Humphrey, *The Seven Lives of John Murray: The Story of a Publishing Dynasty*, London, John Murray, 2009.

Lantern Slides

Page 224

[1] Coloured Lantern slides from the Sir Walter C. Hillier Collection at The Royal Geographical Society (with IBG). Sir Walter C. Hillier (1849–1927) was a distinguished diplomat, academic and, in the later part of his career, Professor of Chinese at Kings College London. Between 1889 and 1896 he was Consul General in Seoul, Korea and became a great supporter and friend of Isabella, writing the preface of her book *Korea and her Neighbours* in 1898.

Contemporary Place Names

Wherever possible we have endeavoured to use the original text from letters, maps and journals, and books by Isabella Bird, or from works contemporary to her, in order to be sympathetic to her original accounts and the period in which she travelled. By doing this we have printed naming conventions that may have been used historically, but which are no longer currently used. To assist the reader, we include below a list of contemporary place names.

Name used by Isabella Bird	Modern name	Administrative division
Amoy	Xiamen	Fujian
Chefoo	Yantai	Shandong
Chemulpo (Korea)	Incheon	Incheon
Chengtu	Chengdu	Sichuan
Chungking	Chongqing	Chongqing
Chusan	Zhoushan	Zhejiang
Foochow	Fuzhou	Fuijian
Fukien (province)	Fujian	
Hangchow	Hangzhou	Zhejiang
Hankow	Hankou	Hubei
Han Yang	Hanyang	Hubei
Hong Kong	Hong Kong	
Ichang	Yichang	Hubei
Kiu-kiang	Jiujiang	Jiangxi
Kuan Hsien	Dujiangyan	Sichuan
Luchow	Luzhou	Sichuan
Mien-chuh Hsien	Mianzhu	Sichuan
Muk-den	Shenyang	Liaoning
Newchwang	Yingkou	Liaoning
Ningpo	Ningbo	Zhejiang
Paoning Fu	Langzhong	Sichuan
Peking	Beijing	
Phyong-yang (Korea)	Pyongyang	
Putu	Putoshan	Zhejiang
Shao-Hsing	Shaoxing	Zhejiang
Somo	Suomo	Sichuan
Swatow	Shantou	Guangdong
Shanghai	Shanghai	
Sui-fu	Yibin	Sichuan
Tientsin	Tianjin	Tianjin
Ting-hai	Dinghai	Zhejiang
Wan Hsien	Wanzhou	Chongqing
Wuking Fu	Songling	Jiangsu

Index

Acknowledgements

Permission to publish from materials in the John Murray Archive is granted by The National Library of Scotland. I owe a great deal of thanks to the library staff, who provided help and assistance in accessing material from the archive.

I would particularly like to thank the following individuals who have assisted me and contributed to my research:

David McClay, John Murray Archive Senior Curator, National Library of Scotland, who provided invaluable help and insights into the archive.

John Murray VII for the provision of the archive, the letters and records of business between publisher and author, and for providing a unique viewpoint on how Isabella Bird worked as a travel writer.

Professor Robert Bickers, University of Bristol, Project Director, and Jamie Carstairs, Digitisation Officer of the Chinese Maritime Customs Project, for providing invaluable help at the beginning of the project by aiding identification of locations via the use of the Historic Photographs of China image database.

Dr Michael Pritchard FRPS, Director General of The Royal Photographic Society, for his help in providing information on RPS membership.

Pamela Roberts, Curator of The Royal Photographic Society (1982–2001), for whom I had the good fortune to work in the 1980s, when she opened up the archive to international institutions and researchers in a pre-internet age.

Because Isabella Bird did not originally intend to publish a book on China, and as her prints came to the Society through her estate, the information on which countries a few of her images where taken in, from her travels in China, Japan and Korea, had become confused. I therefore gratefully acknowledge and thank Weipin Tsai, Lecturer in Modern Chinese History, Royal Holloway, University of London, and Jianing Xu, researcher of Chinese history and early photographic history of China, writer and translator, for their assistance in removing as many of the non-Chinese images as possible for this publication.

Richard Ireland, who read the manuscript and made many helpful suggestions.

Chris and Karen Coe, founders of Travel Photographer of the Year, for their continuing support and encouragement, and for providing the opportunity to work with them, showcasing the history of travel photography.

Richard Wiles, Ian Penberthy and Robin Shields at Ammonite Press for their help and assistance.

Alasdair Macleod, Head of Enterprises and Resources of the Royal Geographical Society (with IBG) and Jamie Owen, Picture Library Sales Manager, whose help was invaluable, supplying information and images, and making available items from the Foyle Reading Room of the RGS-IBG. As well as thanking the present staff of the Royal Geographical Society (with IBG), I would like to acknowledge a debt I owe to the staff from the past, particularly those who worked at the Society in the early 1980s, who inspired my interest in the history of travel photography.

Deborah Ireland

AMMONITE
PRESS

Royal Geographical Society
with IBG

Advancing geography and geographical learning